Shake the Dust Off Your Feet and Walk

Faith, Sobriety,
Self-Discovery, and Healing
A Memoir

onomopoulos

Copyright © 2024 by Gina Economopoulos.

All rights reserved. No part of this book may be reproduced or used in any manner without written permission of the copyright owner except for the use of quotations in a book review. For more information, contact: Gina@GinaEcon.com.

ISBN Paperback: 979-8-9908155-0-6
ISBN Electronic: 979-8-9908155-1-3
Library of Congress Control Number: 2024911755

Publishing Consultant: PRESStinley, PRESStinely.com

Portions of this book are works of nonfiction. Certain names and identifying characteristics have been changed.

Printed in the United States of America.

Gina Economopoulos
GinaEcon.com
Gina@GinaEcon.com

Disclaimer

The author's intent is to offer information of a general nature to help you on your quest for emotional, physical, and psychological well being. In the event you use any of the information in this book for yourself, the author and the publisher assume no responsibility for your actions. This publication is not intended as a substitute for the advice of a healthcare professional.

I dedicate this book to all those feeling hopeless
and trapped in darkness, struggling to find God/a
Higher Power, questioning the meaning of your own life
and the lives of others. Remember this: You are not alone.
Beyond you there is a God, a Higher Power,
guiding you every step of the way. Don't quit.
Shake the dust off your feet and walk. Joy, peace,
and hope await you.

In loving memory of my parents, who gave me life.

*For Danny, whose love gave me a new life of happiness, joy,
and freedom.*

Contents

With a Grateful Heart to God and Appreciation

For the grace of perseverance in shaking the dust off my feet and walking with purpose.

For all those He has placed in my life: family, friends, and situations that have shaped me into the faithful woman I am today.

My friend Eileen, who took my words, my pain, my broken heart, my joy, and my healing, helping me share my life to give hope to many.

The rooms of Alcoholics Anonymous: the fellowship, the service, the tools of the program, and the members who have given me a life beyond my wildest dreams.

For Zora Knauf, my editor, for keeping my story authentic and true to me.

For my publishers, Kristen and Maira at PRESStinely, for their expertise, smooth guidance, and assistance.

For you, my readers, in hope of finding hope, strength, and comfort.

For my partner and best friend, Brian, for his unconditional love, support, encouragement, and acceptance of me as I am.

Jesus looked at them and said,
"With man this is impossible, but with
God all things are possible."
~ Matthew 19:26

Preface

The story that I am sharing is about my journey of healing that came through perseverance, faith, and hope for a better life. I experienced three major traumas that left me in a dark state of mind and spirit. By the summer of 2013, there was no faith, no hope, no love, and no God in me. I felt like I was living in hell. I was at my lowest point and was spiritually, emotionally, and physically empty, devoid of purpose. In March of that year, when I found my fiancé, Danny, dead, that was the last straw. My heart was shattered. I hated God.

Here I was, a former Catholic nun, simply existing without God. I did not know what to do nor think. I was depleted. A relative suggested putting my feelings and thoughts on paper and seeing what God would do. Boy, did God do something. I was finally able to persevere through the pain, suffering, and the unknown.

Back then, if someone said to me, "Ten years from now, you will have a purpose. You'll be free from this darkness, living a happy, joyous, and free life. You'll even share that purpose with others," I would have said, "No way, Jose! Not Gina. Gina was meant to suffer her *whole life!*" That was a perspective that had evolved from the physical problems that manifested in childhood, to the loss of my mother that occurred in my twenties, to the abuse I endured in the convent, up until Danny. In the depths of my heart, at the time, I truly believed there was no way I would ever be happy in this lifetime.

Despite my temporary loss of faith, God has been with me, carrying me through by opening new doors and different, unexpected paths that led me to where I am today—finally at peace within my soul and heart. I live an ordinary extraordinary life today that is filled with faith, hope, love, and God. I do have a purpose to share. My journey and my hope is to help you find peace and hope in yours. If you believe, or even *want* to believe, in new beginnings, in triumph over adversity, and in the power of the human spirit to find healing through faith, please join me. It's all worth it.

Chapter 1

I was born in Syosset, Long Island, towards the end of the Swinging Sixties. As the seventh of eight children, I am the youngest daughter in my family. My large Roman Catholic Greek-Italian family filled our home to the brim with love and support.

My physical and emotional challenges tested that love from the day I was born with an underdeveloped hip socket. This condition required me to be in a body cast for my first year of life. I also inherited osteochondromas from my father. It is a painful and debilitating condition where tumors form on the bones throughout the body. The tumors eventually stopped growing when I reached puberty. I have had at least six surgeries to remove the worst of them.

When I was in sixth grade, I fell off the back of my friend's bicycle. I was hospitalized for eight weeks with a fractured femur. I was in a cast and on crutches for six months after that. While I dealt with these physical problems daily, my seven healthy siblings were excelling at sports and earning respect from their peers.

My bone condition and injury kept me from participating in the sports that made my siblings popular. I never reached five feet in height, and my lack of athletic ability made me feel quite different from my siblings. To try and fit in, I volunteered as a basketball manager for the girl's team and even as a mascot, doing anything to be included. I never complained about my pain and always kept a smile on my face. No one knew what I was enduring. Inside I was in agony, constantly comparing myself to my siblings.

Our family argued like all families, but we always felt safe and secure in warmth and love. There was always fun at Christmas time and other family gatherings. Mom, the Italian one, was the glue of the family. Dad, a hardworking Greek, was the provider.

My father had his own business selling uniforms and equipment to postal workers. Dad's pride, joy, and hard work put all but one of us eight children through college. Michael, my oldest sibling, told him to save his money. He claimed he was already smarter than his teachers. That young man went on to make a success of himself on the top of a mountain in the Ozarks.

Our parents loved us unconditionally, each of us in a unique way. I remember at a high school baseball game the mother of my youngest brother's friend told Mom, "Your son Steven is such a great athlete—a great team player and an all-around nice boy. You must be so proud of him." Now mind you, my mom had Steven when she was 49 years old. He was born healthy, yet I was born with all of these physical problems, despite being seven years older. I carried those "why me" feelings for a long time.

Yet, Mom responded, "I am proud of all my children." It felt good to be included. In her own special way, my mother told me she loved me the same as everyone else. I saw myself as different, but she never did.

As I matured, sad things kept happening. It became my norm. I was in at least six car accidents, had two hernias, and the multiple surgeries and physical limitations I was born with followed me like a dark presence. On the outside, I was a happy, cute little teen who always smiled and was outgoing and friendly. Inside I hurt all the time. I felt like I was the black sheep of the family.

People would call me "Gina Lollobrigida" after an Italian actress my mother admired. That made me feel loved. I relished the attention, something I was always seeking as a child.

I just wanted to be liked and would do anything to fit in. I went as far as partying with the high-school jocks. I always wanted to be part of the crowd and the center of attention. I loved the way alcohol made me feel—secure and loved.

High school on Long Island in the early eighties was a trial for me. My peers wore $90 designer jeans and tons of makeup. I wore hand-me-downs and bargain-rack clothes from Sears. My car was a left-over Chevette from one of my older siblings. There were distinct cliques like the jocks, the preppies, and the dirtbags. I went out of my way to be friendly with all of them. Everybody loved the cute, outgoing little Gina, but there were never any boys breaking down my door for a date. I always felt out of place.

When it was time to go to college, I chose a small party school that my sister went to, Eastern Connecticut State University. I certainly did party but still had the reputation of being "too nice." I hated that label. I hated how I looked. I felt too short, too dark, too hairy. I could not run properly because of my bones and hip, so I never excelled in sports. All the things one needed to be popular were absent. I do have a great smile and am blessed with olive skin that tans beautifully in the summer. Still, the boys kept their distance.

Dad retired in 1987. All the other kids in our family had moved on with their lives, starting families and careers. My mom and dad moved to Harrisburg, Pennsylvania, to be near my sister, Kathie. When I graduated college in 1989 with a degree in social work, I moved in with them and my fifteen-year-old brother, Steven. Having a counseling degree and being a pool shark, I thought bartending would be the perfect job for me. I could give advice using my degree to my customers, make a lot of money in tips, and wouldn't have any paperwork to file at the end of the day. As a social worker, there is a lot of paperwork, not something I was a big fan of. I wanted to remain in a college atmosphere—partying and drinking. I also filled out dozens of applications for work on a cruise ship. I always wanted to be a Julie McCoy from the 1980's television show *The Love Boat*. I loved travel, adventure, socializing, partying, and having fun.

My parents planned to spend winters in Florida after their youngest, Steven, finished high school. They would move there permanently when he graduated college. Everyone was happy for them. They were fulfilling a dream of enjoying their senior years together.

In August of 1991, my mother went to the hospital for minor back surgery. The surgeon discovered she had a rare, malignant form of bone cancer, osteogenic sarcoma, "child's cancer." Fewer than 1 percent of the population gets it. The doctors told us she was terminally ill and only had four to six months to live.

Mom responded in her quiet yet determined way; she was going to fight this cancer. She was determined to be at Steven's college graduation and there for all her children's future events.

Dad and I took care of Mom for five months. We tried everything—prayers, fruits and vegetables said to cure cancer, and even religious artifacts and relics, such as the glove from Padre Pio, a modern-day Italian saint that my Uncle Ralph and Aunt Mel were devoted to. He was known to have performed many miracles and cures to those who asked for his prayers. We also gave Mom different teas like Chinese wood, and we even suggested marijuana. Mom would not partake in marijuana, but she did whatever else we suggested. Mom and Dad were devout Catholics. Mom took out her Italian rosaries and would pray on them. I was not familiar with the rosary nor Our Blessed Mother, yet I figured that these special prayers would heal my mom, so I prayed with her. I was trying everything I could to keep my mom alive. During her sickness, I came to realize moms are special. I kept a daily journal on how mom was doing. One day, my mom asked, "Gina, what are you writing in that small book?"

I told her, "Mom, when you start dancing on the table, we can tell everyone there was a miracle through Our Lady and Padre Pio's prayers." She just smiled.

One month before her passing, she kept saying, "Gina, I want to go home."

My response as a daughter who needed her mother was, "Mom, you are home." I was doing everything in my power to find a miracle. I was hanging on.

One Wednesday afternoon, she asked me again. This time I said, "Mom, you can go home." I didn't realize this would be the last conversation we would have—the last time I would hear her voice. The next moment, she fell into a coma, and that Friday night, she finally succumbed to cancer.

On that freezing cold January evening, my mother was at home in a hospital bed, surrounded with warmth and comfort from six of her children and her faithful husband. We had placed Mom in the television room so that she could greet her family and many friends who walked through the door with her great smile. She had a view of the crucifix on the wall, a picture of Our Blessed Mother by her side, and a rosary in her hand. As her body was failing and riddled with pain, she always smiled and never complained. She looked awful at the end, yet when I looked in her eyes, she was beautiful. I always told her that she was beautiful, even with a bald head and sunken cheeks. Her eyes told a story filled with love for us all.

Michael, my oldest brother, had flown in from Arkansas. He played a sad song he had written, "Now It's Time to Let Go." Steven, the youngest son, saw our mother raise her head and saw a light, and then rested her head by my side with my dad behind me and breathed her last breath at peace as Michael finished the song. At that moment, I felt as if I had died too. *What happened to all those rosaries and prayers to Padre Pio? What happened to the miracle I was hoping for?* I was twenty-five years old. Not only had I lost a mother and my best friend, but I also felt like I had lost a child, being her caregiver at the end of her life.

Chapter 2

There are moments in a person's life that define who they are and foreshadow who they will become. I did not realize it at the time, but when my mother passed, I was devastated. At the funeral, friends and family sympathized, "She is in a better place now. She is with God."

I received all my sacraments and attended Mass regularly right up until I started college. College seduced me into a Sodom and Gomorrah type of life on campus. During that time, I had stopped going to church. After Mom's death, I began to wonder, *Who is this God person that took my mother away?* I was so empty inside. I wanted answers. I wanted to find meaning in this terrible loss.

I began a spiritual journey of discovery. I studied Christianity and tried to understand what sustained a person's faith when all felt lost. Through my searching, I came to know Jesus. The embracing of Christ's Resurrection brought me to the sacraments of the Catholic faith with a fervent enthusiasm.

I swung from a rather wanton lifestyle, with an innocent smile on my face, to warning everyone, in a subtle way, "You are going to Hell if you are not Catholic!" I became a real "Jesus freak." The change in me was radical, from one extreme to the other. My cousin Remo, who was dedicated to the Church, brought me to his parish for every kind of activity—Masses, novenas, retreats, praying the rosary. He was also instrumental in introducing me to the Franciscan Friars he knew.

In August 1993, Pope John Paul II was going to Denver, Colorado, for World Youth Day. Newly returned to the church, participating in daily Mass, rosary prayer meetings, and Eucharistic adoration created an intense desire to be a part of this special Catholic Youth Event. My cousin's connections with the Franciscan Friars and Sisters enabled me to go with them.

Seventeen buses followed one another from Steubenville University in Ohio to Denver for the three-day pilgrimage. That event afforded me the opportunity to bond with the Franciscan religious community. Instead of hanging out with people in a bar, drinking and partying, I was part of a spiritual group. It did not matter what you looked like or how fast you could run, what kind of car you drove or clothes you wore. I had what was necessary to be included in the group of young men and women discerning God's will. We all had the same question to answer: Did God choose us to become nuns, friars, or priests?

Observing these young people whose faith was leading them to Holy Orders, giving their life to God and having fun at the same time, inspired me. I announced, "That is what I think I want to be—a nun."

I did not know anything, really. I just went from one extreme—partying, bartending, and being a pool shark—to donning the habits of a holy roller. Today I can identify how empty I felt inside. I was looking for love and acceptance. I so desperately wanted to be a part of something, to belong somewhere, and the Catholic Church opened its arms to me.

I was fascinated with the concept of vocation. What is a religious vocation? I was taught it is a calling from God, a supernatural grace. A person is called, by nature, to be single, or they may feel marriage is the way for them to serve God. When you receive a calling to religious life as a priest or nun, it is a supernatural grace by God to sustain you through a life of poverty, chastity, and obedience. You dedicate your life totally, with an undivided heart, to belong to God only. Possessing that love and grace, you reach out to your fellow sisters and brothers in the religious community.

You reach out to the poor or youth, or whomever God puts in your life and heart. You pray for them, minister to them, and serve them through God's word. A vocation is a serious undertaking.

One needs to spend time in contemplation, prayer, and sacrifice to know what God's will for them is.

On return from that pilgrimage in Denver, I worked at a retreat house, a very peaceful place in Westchester, from 1994 to 1995. I cooked meals for the priests that lived there as well as lay people who would come on retreat while I tried to figure out God's will for me. In September 1995, while I was contemplating joining the sisters' community, I met a young man. He wanted to be a priest, and I was quite sure I was going to be a nun. As feelings began to come up between us, I suppressed them. I chastised myself, believing that I shouldn't be having these feelings. At the last minute, however, I decided not to join the sisters.

I look back now and see how immature I was. My life experience was limited to my caring family, seeking acceptance from my peers throughout my schooling, and four years at college living the high life of alcohol and partying. I did not know much about feelings, and even though everybody was telling me I had a religious vocation, I was unsure of my faith and calling.

Chapter 3

Instead of joining the sisters in September of 1995, that young man and I went back to Harrisburg and tried dating. We wanted to see if we might better serve God as a married couple. I was needy. I searched for love and acceptance through pleasing others. It did not work out, and I broke up with him shortly afterwards.

In March of 1996, after our breakup, I just wanted to live a simple, normal, and stable life. I was 28 years old with no job, no husband, no white picket fence with children—something I'd always dreamed of. Deep down in my heart, I always wanted to get married and have a big family like my parents did. I did not know if I was being called to be a sister or not, but I was tired of trying to figure out what God wanted me to do. So, after our breakup, I had planned to find a job and continue to live as a lay person.

I got a job in Harrisburg working for a 36-year-old lady, who was disabled. She was in constant pain, and her husband was a blue-collar worker. She was not the easiest person to work for. One cool March morning, I arrived for work at 8:00 AM. There was yellow tape around the house, and the kitchen looked like it had been burning. I rushed home and called the fire department to ask if there was a fire on Mountain Road. They said yes, and that there had been two fatalities. I asked what happened, but they could not tell me anything.

It was on the local news, and I discovered my employer and her husband had been murdered. She had been shot in the head, and the husband had been beaten and stabbed to death. The killer started a fire with a log to cover the evidence. There was no break-in or theft.

I was the last one to see them alive. I had left the house around 4:00 PM the previous day, and they were killed around 7:30 PM. I feared for my own life. Whoever had done this might be after me as well.

The police did not have any leads. I was questioned several times and failed the lie detector test three times. I was a good suspect. I had a key to the house, and I had been honest when I told the FBI that my employer was mean to me. After all the questioning and failing the lie detector test three times, I really thought I might have done it.

Innocence and God on my side kept me safe. My dad and my sister Kathie insisted I talk to a lawyer. The lawyer told me the police were trying to set me up, to pin the murders on me. He counseled me to stop trying to help the FBI. When I was called in to take the lie detector test a fourth time, I told the FBI, on the advice of my lawyer, I was not obligated to take it again. They released me. During this stressful, scary time, I was reaching out to the sisters community for prayers for the souls of my employers as well as those who committed the crime. I ended up visiting the sisters as the investigation was going on. In April, while I was with the sisters during holy week, I felt that God was calling me there. Yet I wondered if it was really a calling from God or if I was just trying to please others since so many of the sisters and friars wanted me to join.

I didn't hear anything more about the case until the Spring of 1998, and by that time, I had joined the convent. When the police heard that, they thought I was running away. That makes me laugh because I know now the only thing I was running from was myself. The FBI came out to the Bronx once to question me. I still looked good as a suspect. They thought I might have been having an affair with the husband. Now that I was a nun, it seemed so preposterous. I chuckled.

The police eventually found the guy who did it. Five years after the crime was committed, I got a call from my sister Kathie confirming the true murderer's capture. He was a friend of the victim's mother. I was told that I would receive a subpoena to go to court, but thank God, guilt finally made him confess, and I didn't have to go.

The motive was money, I believe. When I got the news, I was at the convent and had just gotten out of Mass. Coincidentally, the Mass had been a five-year memorial Mass for the murder victims. I saw it as a sign from God that He was protecting me.

I suffered from stomach-reflux erosion after the murder. Once the stress was gone, however, so was the condition. As a novice, I was also diagnosed with polycystic ovary disease, and the doctor put me on birth control as a treatment for the disease. Ironically, being a sister, I was not planning to have any intimacy with a man, yet it did help at the time. During my novitiate, as I was running on the treadmill, I felt a bone move in my right thigh. My first thought was, *Here we go again. The calcium deposit has moved. Why me?* I was sent to Sloan Kettering to see an orthopedic oncologist, and that's where I learned my bone condition that I inherited from childbirth and had already had several surgeries for could become bone cancer in my later years. By this time, when it came to my physical problems, I had gotten used to it. Not in a cheerful, accepting way, but in a "poor me," "everything happens to me" way.

My health conditions have set me apart from others and have contributed to me developing a poor self-image. I saw myself as a victim, and after the murder, even in my thirties, I continued to feel that everything happened to poor Gina.

Chapter 4

I took three years of contemplation before I actually joined a Franciscan order in New York. In addition to initially thinking I might be called to marriage, being a suspect in a murder case, and general confusion, I questioned whether my devotion to God was just pure loneliness.

The sisters and friars just loved me. How could you not? Wherever I go, whomever I meet, I have "personality plus"—people are drawn to me. I am kind. I smile and I please people. I like to take care of others. I am compassionate, and I endure hardship in silence. I am outgoing because I want so desperately for everyone to like me.

Although I was a member of the Franciscan Sister order for almost twelve years, I always felt like I was treated as an outsider. I saw a great deal and heard more. I was always in the wrong place at the wrong time, it seemed. I always sensed there was an aura of fear and control in the religious community.

There were many secrets, and a great deal of denial about disturbing events in the community. Painful times were never spoken about. There was control, manipulation, and lies so unlike the loving, supportive family in which I had grown up. Yes, I had my faults, but during my years as a nun, I experienced mistreatment, disrespect, and outright emotional abuse.

I tried to protect myself from the hurtful treatment. I reached out to those I thought were friends. I shared my feelings and asked for advice. I questioned, "Why is this happening to me?" to anyone who would listen. It was an extremely grim time in my life.

I loved to pray. I was always in the chapel, praying rosaries, interceding for my fellow man. There were times I was able to spend at least eight hours in the chapel. As Catholics, we believe Jesus is in the Eucharist in the tabernacle. Why would I want to go anywhere else? I felt I was as close to Christ as one of the apostles 2,000 years ago, resting my head on His heart.

That insight was why I stayed in the chapel for hours and hours. I appeared to be the "holy nun," but as my years went on as a sister, it became my safe place, a haven. I found peace in this quiet state until I was reprimanded. I was told I spent too much time in the chapel.

When I entered the religious life, I was loved by all. They were so pleased I had joined them. They thought I was a very pious sister. At first, I was happy. I was giving my life to God. Our community worked with the poor, as well as evangelizing. I loved the poor, and they returned that love in gratitude for the work we did.

I always said yes to everything. "I will do that, sister" was always my answer to my co-nuns. "No" was not in my vocabulary. I do not think it ever was. I wanted to make other people happy, and to avoid confrontation. *What if I was wrong to state my opinions?* I would worry. I was a kind, smiling person, a nun that everyone loved. They all thought I was cute because of my petite size, and that I always smiled and never complained. That was my MO, smile without complaints.

When I entered the order in January of 1997, I was the eighth sister in rank. Sister Maria was the one in charge of the community. In the Franciscan way, she is known as a community servant. It is a humble title as compared to Mother Superior. The servant is known to serve her religious community as well as those to whom we ministered. It was a term that St. Francis used back when he began the order in 1209.

When you join an order, you become a postulant. Usually, we wore jumpers. As part of the community, we lived with the order and took classes on everything from spirituality to the Franciscan way of life. We learned the Catholic catechism and other subjects such as prayer and the life of Saint Francis.

The postulant also helps people outside the community—giving food to the homeless, conducting home visits for shut-ins, really anything to help create a faith-based environment. Postulancy is an aspect of discernment to see if this life is for you. The entire religious community observes you to see if this was a life you had been called to.

Living life as a Franciscan sister is a very austere and simple life. Our cells (bedrooms) were made up of a bed board with a sleeping bag or a thin mattress, a desk, and a chair. On the wall we were allowed a cross and a picture of our Blessed Mother. What we did not have were TVs, couches, radios, computers, cushions, cell phones, microwaves, air conditioners, rugs, or pictures. Everything was simple and made from wood. I was always a simple person, never materialistic, so I did not miss having possessions.

I am easy-going—too easygoing. There were times I was a pushover or a doormat. Most things never bothered me. If something did bother me, I never told anyone. I just kept it hidden. The coping skills I developed in my early life as a response to pain and heartache prepared me for my years as a nun.

For the first few years, I was worried and concerned about whether this life was for me or not. *Will I make it? Will my physical problems get in the way?* I thought my physical problems were part of the suffering I had to endure for the community.

The first summer, wearing the jumper as a postulant, was hot. The old buildings we lived in in the South Bronx had no air conditioning. There was no going to the beach or jumping in a pool.

I always loved the summer. I grew up on Long Island by the beach. Our family had a built-in pool in the backyard. I was always outside with practically nothing on. I never liked to be constricted by clothing in the summer. My summer wardrobe consisted of bathing suits, shorts, and tank tops. What I especially loved about the summer was how dark my tan got. My Greek-Italian olive complexion was my one real vanity. My great tan, I felt, made me look good, and others agreed.

During my postulancy, it was extremely hard to get through the summer. I remember sneaking off and going to the top of the building to tan my face, my hands, and toes. I was strongly tempted to leave. When I expressed my doubt to Father Bonaventure, who was my spiritual director and founder of the community, he quoted scripture, "Jesus says put your hands to the plow, go forward, and don't look back."

Novitiate is a preparation time of penance and sacrifices, a time of letting go of the life you knew before. It is a time of learning and living vows of poverty, chastity, and obedience. As you enter the novitiate, it is more of dying to worldly things and putting on a new self, a new creature in Christ. This new you chooses or is given a new name.

Those in the postulancy with confidence about moving forward to the novitiate would pray for guidance in choosing a new name for themselves. You could keep your baptismal name, you could choose to be named after one of your favorite saints, or you could have the community servant choose your name for you.

As I prepared to enter the novitiate, I was not thinking of a name. My only classmate who was a postulant with me decided to leave the order three weeks before we were to enter the novitiate. I was shocked, surprised, and upset. She was the reason why I wanted to go forward; I really was not sure I wanted to until God gave me a sign. Sr. Maria knew how I felt and insisted that God wanted me there. So, I did not have a preference for my new name, although I had chosen the title of the Immaculate Conception weeks before.

When I asked Sister Maria to choose my name for me, she was hesitant to change it drastically. She knew how I felt, so she decided to keep it as Sister Gina Marie of the Immaculate Conception, just changing my middle name from Nicole to Marie.

As you enter the novitiate, your hair is cut to symbolize leaving the world. A woman's hair is her crown, part of her identity. That bond with personal appearance needs to be broken to give oneself completely to Christ. The hair cutting is a private ceremony, for the community only.

At the last moment, before the cutting ceremony, Sister Maria was inspired by the Holy Spirit to change my name to Regina. I knew it was a truly spur-of-the moment decision because on the celebration cake downstairs they had inserted a cardboard "RE" before the "Gina." So that is how I became Sister Regina Marie of the Immaculate Conception. Regina, meaning queen, is named after Our blessed Mother. It was the beginning of a long and painful period in my life. The queenship I had was one of suffering.

Chapter 5

Within a year, I saw quite a few women leave and new women come in. Before long, I became second-in-charge, Sister Maria's right-hand sister. That is where a relationship of love and hate began. It was mostly based on fear and insecurity—my own as well as hers.

Sister Maria was very meticulous in the formation of the community. It was a brand-new community and imperative that we kept up appearances. We could not look bad to the rest of the religious community or the lay people, especially because sisters were constantly leaving.

I supported Sister Maria and encouraged her. I always believed and trusted that God would work through her. I was obedient to her along with Fr. Bonaventure. I did not doubt them. As I revisit that time, I wonder why so many sisters were leaving before making their vows. It had to have been a red flag that something was seriously wrong with the community.

For instance, one postulant was encouraged to leave because she cut a sandwich wrong for Fr. James. She was accused of being defiant and disobedient and not following the rules. The truth was, Sister Maria did not like her. Sister Maria was always focusing on what the sisters did externally. She looked for any excuse to make them want to leave when she felt they did not fit in. Sister Maria's voice was sweet and tender when she persuaded the sister to leave. She was so manipulative one truly felt leaving was a personal choice and not a banishment. In my opinion, it was a sickness. I suspect that Sister Maria was affected by a crippling and deep-seated insecurity.

When friars or lay people had questions about the actions of our religious community and why so many sisters were leaving,

I always defended Sister Maria. I would claim, "It is what God wants. She is doing what God wants." I would encourage her. I would tell her she was doing a good job. I would tell everyone what a good person Sister Maria was. I wanted to please her. I did not have an opinion of my own. If I did and it was negative, I feared I would be told I was wrong and be reprimanded.

Sister Maria did not yell at me in a high, screaming voice but in a subtle way. When she was upset with other sisters or did not like what they were doing, or did not like *them*, instead of talking to them, she would get upset with me. I got often knocked down emotionally.

I felt I was a victim of what is known as the "First Child Syndrome." I would be the one in trouble. A hardship would be visited upon me, while others received benefits. I had not done anything bad, but I was treated as if I were bad. I perceive it was her reaction to my upbeat personality.

Everyone loved me. I was Sister Regina, the one who smiled. The caring, kind, friendly nun who never said a mean word to or about anyone. Nobody knew what I was going through until it came out 10 years later. Everyone thought Sister Maria and I were best friends, a great team. Sister Maria said she loved me, but I see now it was a false love. The way I was treated, the way I responded, was not real love. There were many examples of this throughout my religious life.

One time I felt deeply hurt by Sister Maria. I shared it with Fr. Bonaventure, my confessor. He told me, "You are suffering for the community," and then he advised me to tell Sister Maria directly. I remember asking her if I could talk to her. We went into the back room off the kitchen.

She knew something was up and asked, "What's wrong?"

I said, "It's you."

I was not a good communicator and had trouble expressing myself. She responded as if I had wounded her. By the end of the conversation, it was all my fault. She left, hurt. Nothing was resolved. I did not have the confidence to stand up to her, to simply be myself.

Because I was living this twisted reality day by day, I did not know that my personality, the essence of who I *was*, was being crushed. It made me question my calling. I agonized; *Do I belong here anymore?* I did not see I was being confused on purpose as a control method. I began to feel I was the crazy one.

I lived two separate lives. One was in the convent, full of fear, walking on eggshells. The other was when I was out serving and helping people. I was more relaxed talking with lay people. I was more myself, more comfortable, when I was not with my own sisters in the convent. I feared I was being watched by the other nuns. After ministering to the neighborhood, upon return to the convent, I would hear that night, or the next day, or even months later that I acted in a manner that was not appropriate. The term disobedience was invisibly written on my habit. The accusations were never to my face, never direct, so I could never defend or clarify my side of the story.

Christmas Eve Mass was always open to family, friends, and the public. Many people come back every year. We would have a beautiful solemn High Mass welcoming the Baby Jesus, and afterwards there was a big celebration downstairs with coffee and desserts. That was when we could greet our families and friends, wishing them a Merry Christmas.

One Christmas Eve, there was a teenager attending whom I had known before I was a sister, when he was 11. Now 16, he had grown into a tall, handsome young man, even though he was still very child-like inside. He saw me and gave me a great big hug and smile, wishing me a Merry Christmas. I hugged him back and thanked him.

Later that night, Sister Maria reprimanded me. She said it was inappropriate for me to be hugged by that boy. I felt the hug had been innocent and sincere. *What was I supposed to do? Reject him? Move away?* I explained he was a kid from the city who did not have a great life, but she still felt it was wrong.

That was an example of what I dealt with on a regular basis. It seemed like I always did something wrong in Sister Maria's eyes. I allowed the criticism without defense. I was resigned to the blame that it was all me. *What was I doing wrong?* I wondered.

Another time, right after I made my final vows, I had been gifted with a couple of fishing poles. I love to fish! I was at a family retreat on Enders Island with Sister Josephine, Fr. George, and Brother Tom. There were seven families, with at least seventeen kids. Each morning, I would get up at 5:30 AM to go fishing with the children. Half would show up each day. We caught buckets full of porgies and kept them for dinner. The last morning, it was a Friday, and no kids showed up. I decided to go and enjoy fishing by myself.

An hour later, Brother Tom came by, "Good morning, sister. Did you catch anything?"

"Yeah, but I threw them back. There is an extra rod if you want to try your luck."

Brother Tom happily grabbed the rod and picked a spot to fish a little distance away. Sister Josephine came along and saw us and said good morning. That was it. We had a nice week of retreat and fishing.

Five months later, Sister Josephine asked to talk to me privately. She mentioned that incident of Brother Tom and I fishing alone. She said it did not look good. It was ridiculous. We were far away from each other, and if you knew Brother Tom, he is the gentlest and most reserved and modest brother. He would never knowingly put himself or anyone else in a compromising situation.

Sister Josephine confessed it had been bothering her; therefore, she told Sister Maria. Sister Maria insisted it was necessary to make me aware of how inappropriate my behavior was. I thought, *Now you say something, five months after it happened?* I felt it was absurd but didn't have the courage to say it.

Fr. Bonaventure and Sister Maria would caution, "Stay away from friars. Make sure two sisters are always together at events and in classes." We would take classes with friars. Instead of teaching us how to relate with friars in an open and Godly way, we were instructed, "You don't want to be like a friar. Sisters want our own identity."

We were always reaching out to the friars for money, for Masses, for handiwork; we needed their help. Sister Maria acted hurt if the friars left us out of an event or did not include our name with theirs. It was crazy, chaotic, and contradictory.

Through all my years as a sister, when I would struggle with a problem or be angry at a sister, I would bring it to Fr. Bonaventure's attention. As my spiritual director, he would say that I was suffering for the community. When I shared my anger, he would convince me it was always my fault. *What is wrong with* me? I wondered.

All the sisters I needed to complain about were under the direction of Fr. Bonaventure. My feelings were stifled and downplayed. I did not know what it meant to be genuinely angry. My feelings of sadness, loneliness, and fear were not recognized. To me, that is not a religious life. I could not be myself. It was a sick community, and I was just as sick because I allowed myself to be subjected to it.

Many times, I wanted to leave the community. I struggled with going to see Sister Maria and Fr. Bonaventure about my concerns. When I found the courage to ask for guidance, they gave the same advice, "You belong here. When God calls you, He will never turn his back on you."

At one point, there were only four sisters that formed the community. One of the four, Sister Catherine, left abruptly after writing an angry several-page letter to Sister Maria. Copies were sent to the Cardinal, Fr. Bonaventure, Fr. Augustine, and Fr. Dominic. Her letter accused Sister Maria of not being equipped to be a servant.

Personally, I thought Sister Catherine was crazy. But there might have been truth to the letter. The blame and responsibility could have been placed on both women, but the whole incident was covered up.

Once Sister Catherine left, there were only three nuns in the convent. Fr. Bonaventure and Sister Maria wanted new girls to come in that September so we would look good. Meanwhile I said, "Let us have a year just for us, to strengthen our foundation. We have been through so much." I also knew most of the girls would not last, and I would suffer for it. However, their primary concern was to look good, and sure enough, they made sure three postulants entered that September. Within two and a half years, they were all gone, off to get married, and I was made to suffer for it once more.

I had no idea at the time, but years later, a therapist introduced me to the concept of the scapegoat. With the sisters, she saw me as a "scapegoat"—one that is beautiful, that stands out, but the community sacrifices for their own sins and wounds. She explained in ancient history, the tribe would choose the most beautiful, kind women to be sacrificed, to be killed for the sins of the community.

Usually, the scapegoat was oblivious to their intentions until she was made to experience pain, suffering, and even death. Later, instead of humans, they would choose the fatted calf, not the skinny one, for sacrifice. She pointed out how I was the scapegoat for that community—beautiful, well loved by many, good, loving, and silent about my suffering.

The other sisters benefited from my position, and it justified their own defects of jealousy and envy. I received the brunt of it all. I felt Sister Maria really did not like me or was jealous of me. At a meeting with me and two other nuns, she voiced it aloud. Sister Maria stood up, pointed at me, and hissed, "The friars like you better."

Up until that point nobody dreamed that the relationship Sister Maria and I had was anything but friendly and loving. Sister Veronica told me that it was not right for her to say that to me.

I was being depleted and was put down repeatedly. Anytime I tried to be honest, somehow it was twisted until I was doing something wrong. I was forever sticking up for Sister Maria, with the friars as well as the lay people. With the help of the sisters and friars, I even threw her a surprise birthday party to lift her spirits when she was discouraged and at a low point. I never wanted anyone, especially Sister Maria, to be hurt. I was just as sick as she was. I allowed myself to go through it all with her, taking on her pain as if it were my own.

I made final vows on August 2, 2003, feast of our Lady of the Angels. I was the first one of the professed sisters in that new community to make it through. It had been such a long time since a sister made final vows, no one knew what the protocol was. The community planned the ceremony in August so my family could come. I sent out eight hundred invitations—with an Our Lady of the Angels picture in front of the invitation. I knew a lot of people! Family, friends, those we served. Three men from the homeless shelter chipped in and brought me a dozen red roses. I was deeply moved. I wanted everyone to witness my wedding day—the day I married my God. I chose an extra title for my name. From that day forward I was named Sr. Regina Marie of the Immaculate Conception and the Holy Souls in Purgatory. During my time in the convent, the Holy Souls became my friends. I had a great love for the souls that had passed away and spent a great deal of time praying for them.

I remember the day of the event, my cousin Remo came up to me and said, "Are you sure you want to go through with this?" He saw me struggling. He sensed that I was unhappy. He knew the community, and as an outsider, he felt it was unhealthy. I could not share the details of my struggle with him, and he never knew how right he was. I just kept smiling and saying, "Yes."

Chapter 6

After making final vows, I was assigned to be the servant and postulant director at a convent in the North Bronx, while Sister Maria remained servant of the community, overseeing the novices at a second location a few miles away.

Everyone at my new assignment loved me. The friars loved me. I was told so many times I was more approachable than the other sisters. The other nuns appeared to be overly pious, judgmental, aloof. I was more sociable like the friars. As the servant, I was trying to bridge the gap between friar and sister. To act as an example of caring for one another on a united front. The friars were a much larger group. Many of them were my friends as well as brothers to me. They would say things like, "Why can't more sisters be like you?"

I extended invitations to them to come to Mass or Holy Hour dinner. We would have a fun time praying, laughing, and singing. Sister Veronica thought it was a promising idea. Of course, Sister Maria did not. I guess she didn't trust me because from then on, she instructed me to write down everything we did in the convent daily. I was walking on eggshells, even with her not living under the same roof.

I had to report things like who came over and what was going on in the convent. Every Friday I would fax it to her. I was hesitant and fearful about what I wrote. I could not judge her moods nor predict her response to information I supplied her. I lived in fear of her critical nature, knowing she would visit her anger and judgment upon me no matter what I wrote.

One time, Brother Mike told Sister Maria how he enjoyed teaching the postulants the *Lectio Divina*, which is a contemplative way of reading the Bible. When she heard this news, she claimed to be upset because she had not been informed ahead of time.

"It was on the paper that I fax to you weekly," I assured her.

"Oh, I do not read that. I am too busy. No one knows my burdens or understands my responsibilities." Her response was typically dramatic and full of self-pity.

When Sister Veronica made final vows, Sister Maria assigned her to replace me as servant and director. These were positions I had held for two years. I was demoted to second-in-charge. The other sisters appeared to be sympathetic, but they were just as quick to stab me in the back.

Deep down, it was Sister Maria's fear that the community would fall apart, I believe. Something like that had happened once before, in the first years of the community. The community had a cookie-cutter template. If you fit the mold, everything would be fine. If not, you would be encouraged to leave, or be treated in a way that would make you want to leave.

Sister Maria aimed her emotional double-barrel shotgun right at my most vulnerable area: my need to be loved, to be accepted, to be a part of a community that needed me. The constant harassment was like stones building a prison around me. The last eight years of my religious life I was in constant fear. I shared my anxiety with certain friars, as well as in confession with a priest. I remember sharing my situation with Fr. Dubay. I wrote him a letter and asked why Sister Maria was so hard on me.

My mind searched for answers outside of reason. *Is it because I am Italian and from New York?* I honestly thought that might be it; that is how crazy I had become. I explained my predicament to Fr. Dubay on a community retreat and shared that Fr. Bonaventure was my spiritual director as well as advisor to the other sisters. He said he could not give me guidance in matters that included them. Yet, Fr. Dubay encouraged me to find another director outside of the community. I found a Jesuit priest through a mutual connection. When I asked Sister Maria about switching spiritual directors, she told me, in that sweet, sweet voice of hers, "Fr. Bonaventure is a holy priest. It would be sad to switch. Talk to him and see what he suggests."

I presented my case and asked for his blessing to seek outside counsel. At first, he said no, without explanation. The next meeting with him, he changed his mind and said, "Yes." It seemed like nothing was ever gained without a struggle.

When I went to see Fr. Koterski, he encouraged me to start over with the sisters. "Form boundaries. Be yourself." But I found it hard to be myself among the sisters. I felt like I was under a microscope.

After three months of meeting with my new spiritual director, I was beginning a new life of being true to myself. That does not happen overnight. I was learning to love others without fear of being vulnerable or of being reprimanded, as well as obedient. I was learning to be true to myself, to share my feelings and thoughts without fear and worry, and to redevelop my personality without being hurt. I needed to correct certain things, but in a self-loving way. For the other nuns everything was about appearances, following the rules to perfection rather than with compassion. It was more important that our lives set a standard that looked good rather than was good.

In reflection this scenario was bizarre, but at the time, I was in the middle of it. The situation itself did not seem strange. It caused me to question my purpose. So many times, throughout my religious life, I wanted to flap my wings. I wanted to leave. Every time I brought it up, it was like calling to a canyon that echoed, "You belong here. God wants you here. When He calls you, He will never let you go."

It was February of 2006 when I started counseling with Fr. Koterski. On May 31, 2006, the feast of the Visitation, I had a meeting with Fr. Bonaventure, Sister Maria, Sister Veronica, and Sister Ignatius at St. Josephs in Yonkers. The front room of the church was staged for an interrogation with one seat on one side and four on the opposite side. I was directed to sit in that one seat. Later, when I mentioned my feeling of being disciplined, Sister Maria insisted it was not like that.

The first thing Sister Maria said was, "We need a break from you." I was completely floored. I had thought the meeting would be about the upcoming summer. I had been planning to try to have more courage, to be myself, the "new me."

I was wrong. In hindsight their suggestion of needing a break was something more serious. Deep in my heart, I knew they wanted me out. From that moment on, living there was hell for me. It was over two years before I eventually left.

At that meeting they said they wanted me to go away for two weeks, alone, to discern if God's will for me was to be a nun. The panel told me I could choose my fate: go to a religious rehab in Michigan for three months or go to the austere Missionaries of Charity, Mother Teresa's order, in Tijuana, Mexico.

I was already years into final vows, committed with a ring, married to God forever. I thought, *Yes, God wants me here. All these years you kept telling me, encouraging me to stay. As my superiors you are the Voice of God, and I trusted you. After putting my blood, sweat, and tears into my vocation, you are now sending me into exile.*

I felt these words with every fiber of my being. It hurt me emotionally and spiritually as deeply as my bone condition and all the surgeries I had endured. I never had the courage to speak of my pain. I was afraid of the repercussions, the unkindness that would be visited upon me. To speak up, to say or do anything in my own defense, would have been seen by the community as wrong.

No matter what I chose, their intent was clear. The community wanted me gone for at least three months so they could have a break from me. I was shocked. I did not know what to think. I said that I would do it, but I was crushed on the inside.

Sister Veronica, whom I had always thought of as a good friend, revealed her true self. She was not my friend. Anyone who wants you to be untrue to yourself or others is not a friend. When you share your hurt and pain with someone and you feel like you are being judged, they are not your friend. When a peer talks to you like a counselor or treats you like a patient, that's not a friend. When you share your feelings and they keep theirs hidden, that is not a friend.

Sister Veronica tried to be in the middle, but when choosing right from wrong, she chose to be loyal to Sister Maria. During that meeting, they each insinuated that something bad had happened to me as a child of which I was not aware. In my mind and heart, I knew I had a beautiful family and a healthy upbringing. Instead of defending my family life, I said I would take their suggestion into consideration. When my family found out about this, my oldest brother, Michael, had a meeting with my family and chuckled, "Who put Gina in the closet when she was young?"

Chapter 7

That night I packed a car with food and my few belongings and went straight up to St. Clare's. It was the sisters' hermitage, a Cape Cod house in upstate New York. The plan was to go there for a week and the second week to go to the Bethlehem sisters in Livingston Manor. These sisters were real hermits.

I was in deep shock and fear. In tears I recounted my life's journey. I had given up my life that could have given me my own home, a husband, and children. I put all that away and dedicated myself to the religious community. My reward for dedication to my convent was banishment.

I had really loved being a nun, serving people and sharing Jesus with everyone I met. I was called to speak in public forums. I was earning a reputation both in the Catholic and secular world that had started when I made my first vows in December of 1999. That was the day Fr. Bonaventure loosened up the audience with, "Did you know Sister Regina used to be a bartender and a pool shark?"

It captured everybody's attention. I was asked to be on *Life on the Rock*, a worldwide Catholic show for young people on EWTN. On November 2, 2000, I appeared on the show. Sister Maria was with me. Watching the show, one can see my fear intensify when we are together. I am unable to be myself, always watching what I say or do. I never wanted her to get mad nor leave her out. I felt like I was being watched; that I was not behaving properly as Franciscan sister. I was very approachable as a sister, and from her words and unloving responses towards me, I felt she did not like that. No one had any idea what a hardship that was for me, having her there. When EWTN heard I was making final vows, they came to video it. On September 11, 2003, I was on the show again, this time with Sister Ignatius and Sister Josephine.

I was well-known, approachable, well-liked by many—the youth, gangs, elderly, homeless, the shut-ins, lay people, and the friars. Everyone loved Sister Regina—everyone except her own sisters. The sisters loved me the way they loved pizza. I felt their affection was shallow and hollow.

Fr. Dominic, one of the founders of the friars, heard about my situation—that I had been asked to go alone for two weeks to pray and discern. His first response to Sister Maria was "Are you crazy? Sending her up there alone with no one, after what you said to her?"

Two days later, Sister Maria, in her sweetest tone, called and asked if I would like her to come up and be with me. I am sure she had been advised to call me by Fr. Bonaventure. I was sad and underneath it all, *truly angry*. I simply answered, "No, you don't have to." They were acting from an unhealthy system filled with mixed messages. I was not equipped on the inside to do or say anything in my own defense against such emotional abuse.

I was compliant, had made final vows, lived in commitment, and was married to my God. I would do anything to stay. After rivers of tears and non-stop prayers, I chose to go to Michigan for psychological treatment. I decided to embrace the possibility of healing. It is a place where I could talk, share my feelings, and work on myself. I always knew I had low self-esteem and that I did not like myself. I thought this might help me.

Our next meeting at St. Joseph's was June 14, 2006. I left the hermitage two days early, but I was sidelined to Rosary Hill Home in Hawthorne, New York, to stay with the Dominican sisters until our meeting.

The Hawthorne Dominicans are a religious order that works with the elderly and the dying. People in the final stages of life were sent there by their families. The nuns were mostly nurses wearing a habit. I stayed there for a couple of days.

Sister Maria was sickly sweet in our communications, and I found myself stuck in the ooze. While I waited to come home, I spoke with Fr. Koterski, and we both agreed I should go to Michigan.

For the meeting at St. Joseph's, this time, all the chairs were in a circle. I announced my decision to take the trip to Michigan. They were all so happy. Sister Veronica said, "Oh, how I wish I had three months to go away to work on myself!" I thought to myself, *What a stupid thing to say! Does she think this is some kind of vacation for me?*

Sister Maria said she would contact the facility, and that I should be going by next week. As we were leaving, I expected to be able to return to my convent duties. Sister Maria said, "Oh, no. Stay at Hawthorne until you go to Michigan. It should only be a week."

I agreed and asked if I could come over for Holy Hour and dinner. She said, "Yes. I will let you know." The committee left in one car. I had no choice but to drive myself back to Hawthorne, a place that was not my own religious family. I never did go back to the convent for Holy Hour and dinner, and it was almost four months before I was allowed to go to Michigan.

During those months of waiting at Hawthorne, it was delay after delay, one deception after another. When Sister Maria called the center for the first time, they said there was a set of questionnaire forms that needed to be filled out.

They wanted to know what needed to be worked on, from my point of view and from the community's. Once completed, those forms needed to be sent back right away to meet the deadline of the next opening on July 11. Once they got the papers, they would call me for a phone interview with one of the sisters who did counseling at the facility.

We got the papers at the end of the week. When Sister Maria brought them to me at Hawthorne, she also gave me a schedule that I needed to follow during the interim. I was to stay with the Hawthorne sisters until my application was accepted. I was to pray, work, and eat with the nuns as a member of their community.

My assignment was ministering and helping terminal patients. One patient passed while I was praying the rosary with her. Feeling as if I were dying on the inside kept me from seeing the possibility that this was part of my calling, a calling that would become clear to me later in life when I became an end-of-life doula.

I was hurting, always in tears and angry about my predicament. There was a young woman, a friend of the Hawthorne community who lived around the corner from their convent. I would walk to her house just to have someone to talk to. It was a safe place to cry and share what was going on. I did not think there was anything wrong with that, but as soon as Sister Maria found out, she put the kibosh on our visits.

At first, Sister Maria gave me permission to call certain friars, friends, and my family to tell them I was going to Michigan. She hoped it would appear as if I were going to get help voluntarily. This way no one would point a finger at the sisters. I was in pain, confused, and paralyzed by what was happening to me. It broke my heart that not even one of the sisters reached out to me except Sister Maria, and by this time, there was no love there. Fr. Bonaventure resided at St. Joseph's Friary, which was only 15 minutes from Hawthorne, but he did not come to see me. My only visitor was Sister Maria when she came to drop off papers or pick them up, or to impose more restrictions on my behavior. She would bring written instructions and have me sign them.

As the word about my situation got out to the friars and certain lay people, there was an uproar. Sister Maria became convinced I was telling people things that changed their attitudes towards the sisters. She felt people were no longer talking to them, or were ignoring them, or were talking about them behind their backs. I believe that Sister Maria suffered from a form of paranoia, and that her fears intensified all that summer.

She took away my permission to make phone calls to anyone, including my family. Sister Maria used the excuse, "What would they think of us? They do not understand religious life." She believed those outside the convent simply did not understand. Friars and lay people saw my treatment was wrong, but no one stood up for me.

There was Fr. John, but he was out of town at the time. I was waiting for him to come back to share with him, but Sister Maria forbade it. I had asked for permission to call Fr. John, but Sister Maria said no. Because of my vows of obedience, I was expected to comply with her wishes.

In truth, I was still quietly reaching out to certain friars and friends, as well as my family. I felt so abandoned, so lonely, so hurt. All I wanted was a friend. No one had to choose sides; I just desperately needed a friend.

When Sister Maria forbade me to make any more phone calls, she said in her sweet voice, "If you need to talk to someone, you can call Fr. Bonaventure or myself."

My bitter response was, "I don't feel love from either one of you." I was surprised that it came out of my mouth. My response would usually be, "Okay," yet I was filled with anger, sorrow, and pain and did feel completely unloved by my own community.

The forms arrived, and I immediately went to work on them. It was hard to fill them out, but I was as honest as I could be. Two days later, when I completed them, I called Sister Maria, hoping she was finished with hers. We needed to mail them quickly so I could go for the July 11 opening. She was not done with her set of forms. She was waiting for Sister Veronica and Sister Ignatius to return from wherever they were for their input. She kept reassuring me. "Do not worry. It will be done. You will be going July 11." I believed her, and that was part of my problem. I *always* believed her.

It was not until the Friday before the Fourth of July that she finally completed everything. She came up to Hawthorne, and we went over their part of the form. She wrote what she thought I needed to change, what to seek help for, what she and the two sisters saw as my defects, and what I needed to work on. I had to read it with her so I could sign it. She signed it too. It was not actually mailed out until Saturday, July 1.

She continued to assure me that I would be going on July 11, and there was no need to worry. I believed her. I hoped she was right, and that it would happen right away. I was in agony waiting.

I received permission to go and spend the Fourth of July with my sister Kathie, her husband, Kenny, and my family at Kueka Lake, in the Finger Lakes region of Western New York. Years later, I would come here again—a broken, lost soul in need of healing. This is where God is for me. In the sunrise and the sunset, the scenery, the lake itself—all peaceful and all beautiful. It is a slow-paced life. Sailing, time with family, treasure hunts, sun on your face, and cool waters to dip into. It will always have a special place in my heart.

Since I was at the lake, I was afraid I might miss the phone call for the interview. I was sure I would be accepted that week. Sister Maria reassured me not to worry. I could always call the facility myself. On Monday, July 3, I called. Someone named Debbie answered. I tried to explain to her that I was ready for my interview. I insisted they should have received the forms and described my situation as desperate.

She had no record of having received the forms and instantly said, "Oh, no, you will not be coming July 11—that spot is already taken. There will not be another until the end of August." When I heard that, my mouth dropped open. I was enraged. I told my sister Kathie the news as I sobbed tears of frustration. I called Sister Maria. A novice answered and said she was not there. Sternly I commanded, "Please have her call me immediately!"

When she called me back, Sister Maria had every excuse in the book that it was not her fault. She was already planning another schedule for me geared to the longer time in Hawthorne. Finally, she added that if I wanted to contact her, I would have to fax her. I was not to call the convent, because the novice that took my message became afraid when she heard my voice. That broke me. I was completely defeated. I felt like I was a dog on a chain. *I must have done something terrible to deserve this, but what?*

There were friars and friends who secretly came to visit me when I returned to Hawthorne. Sometimes they would even sneak me out. I was in tremendous emotional pain. I did not smile anymore and carried my sadness in the lines etched on my face. I kept praying and praying. I would go into the chapel and pray the stations of the cross in agony, uniting my suffering with that of Jesus. I had nowhere to turn. Psalm 130 said it all:

"Out of the depths of my heart I cry out to you. Lord, hear my cry."

I was not angry with God, but I was very confused. Here I thought I was part of a religious family. We were taught as novices, and it was always stressed throughout our training, that we in the convent were family. "Be charitable to your sisters." *What kind of "charity" was this that caused so much pain? What was going on?* I was not making excuses. I did not want to hurt anybody. I was just trying to survive, looking to be loved by those to whom I had committed my life.

On one occasion I was sitting in the chapel. It was around 9:00 PM. A sister came to me to tell me I had a phone call. It was Fr. John. I was so dead inside that when I picked up the phone, I said, "Sorry, Father. I cannot talk to you."

He said, "I got permission from Sister Maria to call you. She also gave me permission to see you. Can I come tomorrow for dinner and talk?"

That pulled me out of my funk for a minute. In grateful tears, I said, "Yes."

When I saw him the next evening in a room that the sisters gave us to use, I was in tears. He is a big, big, big guy. I gave him a hug, and my head only came up to his armpit. I cried and cried and blurted out my pain. He listened. He said he came to me as a friend. He could not do anything about the situation because neither he nor the friars were in control—the sisters were.

He had been informed this whole situation was Fr. Bonaventure's baby. Nobody wanted to step on anyone's toes. But he did say the friars loved and cared about me and were angry. They had voiced their complaints and anger to him.

The friars encouraged me to speak up. They suggested I go to the Cardinal, the Vicar of Religious Life, to report what was happening to me. Under Canon law, I think I had the right. Unfortunately, I was not equipped with enough courage to fight this. I did not see the full picture. I still did not understand why holy people would treat someone so badly. How could the Franciscans, a well-known, well-loved order in the Catholic world, allow such behavior towards one of their own family.

Fr. John came to visit me a couple more times. He questioned Sister Maria and Fr. Bonaventure, "Is this necessary, to isolate Sister Regina?"

Sister Maria could never give him a straight answer. She was very insecure, full of fear. Most times, she did not know what to do. She told me later that she suffered much during that summer because of me. Only she, Sister Ignatius, and Sister Veronica knew what was happening. She kept it a secret. Everyone—friars and friends—was terribly upset and angry at the sisters.

I found no support from the priests I had respected. Fr. Bonaventure, my spiritual director, told me, "If my name goes down because of this, it will be all your fault."

Fr. Dominic, another founder of the community, told me, "We need to brush this under a rug; nobody needs to hear about it."

When I reached out to Fr. Augustine, whom I thought was a good friend, one that I had known before I was a sister, he said, "I don't want to get involved."

All I said was, "I do not need you to be involved. I just need a friend."

One summer morning, right after Mass, I was in my room at Hawthorne, just crying. I was in such darkness it was scary. I felt rejected, isolated, abandoned, lost. When I was in this desperate state, I had a strange but authentic experience. During those moments feeling alone, I felt the presence of two priests I had known that had committed suicide in the year past. I felt and experienced their pain. I understood why they chose to take their own lives. It's scary feeling that way, but I didn't blame them. At that moment, I was screaming, crying out to God to help me. I was not going to take my own life, but the pain was indescribable. I could see the Devil enter in and say, "Do it." But God is all-merciful. Just when I was screaming out and scared, my name was being called over the intercom. There was a phone call for me. I had so little strength, but I got up to my feet and went to answer it.

That call was my saving grace. It was one of my remaining friends, Fr. Bob, telling me to call a woman named Irene because she might be able to help me out of this limbo and that I might be able to go on a pilgrimage to Medjugorje. I did not tell Father about the eerie experience I had just gone through. I was still too shaken up, so I just said, "Thank you. I will call her."

Irene is a friend of Fr. Bob as well as the other friars. They do a number of ministries at her church in Hamilton Square, New Jersey. I did call her and shared my situation. She told me her husband was going to Medjugorje in August. If I could get permission to go with his group from my superior, she knew someone who would pay my way.

As sisters and friars, we took the vow of poverty and lived lives of Divine Providence, entrusting that God would provide for our financial and material needs. I called Sister Maria—she had removed the phone restrictions and the fax accounting by then— and asked her if I could go. I suspect that after all that had gone on, she would have done anything for me to make herself look good. She gave me permission right away.

I wanted to leave the convent and just give up, but I knew if I did, my next residence would be the psychiatric ward in a hospital. At this point, I didn't know if I was crazy or not. It seemed like everything was all my fault, and what the community was doing was somehow justified.

The night before we went, I really did not want to go. I was so depleted, so down. Once again, Fr. Bob encouraged me to go and be renewed. He pointed out that when I returned was soon enough to decide my future.

Chapter 8

In mid-August, I departed with sixteen other pilgrims. Fr. Timothy was our spiritual director. I had known Fr. Timothy for years through the other friars, and he was shocked to hear what was going on with me and the sisters. He thought the way they were managing it was bizarre.

On the trip, I wore a fake smile, but I was not a happy nun on the inside. I kept it all to myself. I was filled with fear and insecurity and felt very unloved. I was emotionally bankrupt. By this time my physical conditions were nothing compared to what I felt emotionally

During that week in Medjugorje, I did have a profound experience. Medjugorje is a place in Croatia where the Blessed Mother has allegedly been appearing since 1981. Although the Vatican continues to investigate, no official approval has been forthcoming about the authenticity of the claims. However, healings, spiritual awakenings, and conversions have taken place there. There were a number of people who saw the sun spin, rosaries turn gold, and miraculous images appear in photographs. It is a mystical place. I had witnessed those miracles.

This was my third time there, but the first time as a religious sister. Italians, Germans, Irish, Americans—people from all over, really—gather for a time of retreat and pilgrimage, penance, and prayer. It was no vacation.

People of all ages visit the holy shrine, too. I ended up meeting a youth group from Long Island. One of the mothers, Rosemary, was a chaperone, and they had two priests as their directors. I knew one of them—Fr. Tony happened to be my parish priest growing up in Syosset, at St. Edward's Church. He led my confirmation retreat and had performed the marriage ceremony for my sister JoAnn and her husband, Rich, in 1982.

Rosemary knew one of the visionaries, Ivan, very well. He is godfather to one of her children, so they were all staying with him. He had a chapel in his backyard where every night at 6:00 PM he would pray the rosary with those he invited. At 6:40 PM, the Blessed Mother would appear to him, and everyone would stop. She would give him a message. Once she left, he would relay the message for all to hear, then continue to pray the rosary.

On August 15, 2006, the Feast of the Assumption, Rosemary invited me to be part of the rosary at Ivan's house. I sat in front of the chapel with Rosemary. When Our Lady appeared, we fell to our knees and I closed my eyes, asking Our Lady to help me. All I felt was a presence of peace when she entered the room. That was it.

The next morning, I saw Rosemary at church with her youth group. She approached me and invited me back to the chapel that night. She said, "It was not I that invited you; it was Ivan." That day mostly everyone went to see Fr. Joso in the next town over to hear him talk and to be prayed over. Fr. Joso was the priest of St. James Church in Medjugorje when the six children had a vision of Mary in 1981. Since then, he had been the target of persecution and was moved to another church for his own safety. He is a holy priest with so many spiritual gifts of prophecy and healing.

In the hot, open arena with thousands of pilgrims, I was still in my own world of pain and hurt. I kept praying to God and asking Our Lady to intercede for me. I did not know what to do, or what lay ahead for me. I wanted to be a sister so badly—I had committed my life to it. Going through this trial and tribulation, I could only put one foot in front of the other and keep moving forward.

After Fr. Joso gave his talk, he prayed over all the priests and said, "Now go forth and pray over God's children." Of course, I went directly to Fr. Joso. As a nun dressed in my habit it was easy to get through the crowd. Fr. Joso prayed over me in his own language, Croatian. I did not know what he said, I simply accepted his blessings.

Heading back to our bus to go back to Medjugorje, I saw Fr. Tony and asked him to pray over me. I was seeking all the graces I needed from God. He prayed in English, and what came out of his mouth sent me into tears. He was asking for God to give me peace, to light up the darkness in my time of need, to be healed from the hurt of rejection. Everything he said and prayed for over me was what my heart felt and had been experiencing. When he was done, I looked up at him and said, "How did you know?"

He answered, "I do not know. It is very ugly. All I see is something pushing you out." *Exactly.* Hearing those words was what I felt. I was being pushed out by my community.

As soon as we got back to the village, I grabbed a cab and went straight to Ivan's house, to his chapel. We were all running late. I made it there just before the rosary began. When I walked in, the chapel was filled with priests. On Thursday nights, he welcomed the priests by invitation. I found myself sitting behind three rows of priests. But I was not thinking about where I was. My mind and heart were still on what Fr. Tony had said to me.

I was crying on the inside when Fr. Charles began the rosary and asked if I would lead the fifth decade of the Glorious Mysteries—the Coronation. I said yes. We began. Rosemary came in and sat right next to me. I led the fifth decade. Right after that, it was 6:40 PM, the time that Our Lady allegedly appears to the young children daily. Everyone went, "Shush." There was silence. Everyone was on their knees. We heard Ivan whispering to Our Lady. This time I opened my eyes to see, but the heads of the priests in front of me were blocking my view. Then something inside me said, "Look at the cross."

There was a beautiful crucifix behind the altar, the only thing I could see clearly. I poured my heart out to Our Lady, asking for everything that Fr. Tony had been praying for me. As I stared at the cross, a bright light shone from it. I rationalized since it was still bright and sunny out that someone had come through the door and let the sunlight in.

Right after seeing and thinking that, everyone made the sign of the cross, signifying Our Lady had left. Ivan shared the message he had received from Our Lady. He said it in Croatian, but there was an English translator. The message is usually the same: "Pray,

pray, pray for my children, for conversion of sinners, pray the rosary." But at the end of this message, he said, "As our Lady was leaving, she lit up the cross." Rosemary wrote everything down in shorthand, except for the last message, *she lit up the cross*.

Later I turned to her and asked, "Did you see that light?"

She said no and added, "In fact, no one else in the chapel saw it, just you."

What does this mean for me? That I will know suffering for my whole life? That is how I perceived and felt my vision.

I shared my experience when it was over. I saw Fr. Charles and asked him to pray over me. The way I felt, the more prayers and graces, the better off I would be. He saw the same darkness around me as Fr. Tony. He prayed for the graces to help me persevere through this darkness. My shocked response was, "How did you know?"

He said, "I did not. It is what God showed me."

Only Rosemary really knew what was happening with me. I asked her if she had said anything to anyone. She said no. By the end of the week in Medjugorje, I felt strengthened. *Yes*, I thought, *with God's help I can keep going through this.*

Chapter 9

When I returned to the States, I stayed with Irene and her family in New Jersey. I called Sister Maria to see if, and hopefully to hear that, I would be heading to Michigan by the end of August. She informed me that it would not be until October or November. I was okay hearing the news because I had just gotten back from Medjugorje. The question that concerned me now was: *Where do I go in the meantime?*

Sister Maria did not want me back at the convent. She was afraid I would influence the other sisters. Everything was hush, hush, simply to protect the sisters. Sister Maria was trying to look good, to be kind, to accommodate me. I believe in her mind and heart she felt she was doing the right things. Instead of staying in Hawthorne for the remaining, unknown time until Michigan, I was allowed to stay with Irene and her family.

Irene is a loving, beautiful person. She is the mother of three, two daughters and a son. Her son is severely autistic, a very handsome, big boy that cannot talk or express his needs. He is known as Sammy.

He and I became friends. Everybody loves Sammy, but he is fussy and selective about those he loves or will allow to come near him. His head is three times the size of mine. Looking at pictures, you would never think he was severely autistic. He is his own kind of wonderful.

I helped Irene out with Sammy, with housework, and with whatever else needed to be done, to occupy my time until I got the message to go to Michigan. I was surrounded with love, freedom, and support.

At the end of August, I got a call saying I would be going to Michigan on October 3, 2006. Finally, my departure was secured.

I was scared, tired, and depressed. I knew I needed to go, no matter what my future held.

I arrived in Michigan on Tuesday, October 3, the day before the community celebrates the Solemnity of St Francis. A familiar priest I had met once through the convent was my driver. My fear kicked in because I was driving alone with a priest. Nuns were not allowed to be alone with a friar or any man. Another sister must be with you, especially in the car.

My anxiety over the trouble this could cause was not as powerful as my need to get to my destination. Apparently, no one else thought anything of it. Once I got there, I was led to my accommodations. I stayed in a little cottage the size of a garage right next to the main house. There were sisters already there as patients. One other sister came the same day as I did.

Three months of intensive therapy began the next day. I had to take all these psychological tests, followed by group therapy. That is where I heard the rules: confidentiality and the need to respect each other, not only there but when we left. Everyone, everything, those we saw, spoke to, or shared with, stayed in Michigan. Even if I crossed paths with a sister later in life, we could not disclose where we knew each other from. I could tell people where I had been if I wanted to, just not identify anyone else who was there.

There were five of us patients. After hearing the rules, we heard each other's stories. One sister had already completed her program and was leaving the next day to resume her duties at her convent. She shared why she was there, the tools she learned, and how she planned to use those tools. There was a change in her, she told us. She now had the confidence to go back as a sister. She reflected on her three months at the facility and how it had helped her.

When it was my turn to share my story, I felt safe in this room to share my pain. I was in tears. There was no smile on my face when I arrived there. Dr. Teresa, a psychologist sister, said I looked like a wilted flower and assured me that over these next months, they would help me to blossom.

My weeks ahead would consist of the following: Monday, Tuesday, and Thursday we had chores in the morning. In the afternoon was our therapy session, seeing Sister Teresa, the psychologist, Sister Gabriel, a therapy counselor, or Fr. Francis, another counselor. Every Wednesday would be our group therapy, and Friday was a day off. Saturday was chores all day, and Sunday was observed as a holy day of rest. We joined the community for prayer and Mass daily.

The third day I was there, Sister Teresa came and talked to me. I cried and shared more on how hurt I was by the community and what had taken place. Sister Teresa empathized, "You are part of an unhealthy community. We cannot help them, but we will help you by building your insides." She pointed to my heart. I thought, *Everyone sees what is wrong, but nobody wants to talk about it.*

Over the next three months, I worked on myself. The first month they did not have a clear concept of what Sister Maria wanted. They did not know what to do with me. I ended up staying an extra month, with my permission. During this time, I found out that I had an autoimmune deficiency, brought on by the cold. One cold morning in Michigan, as I was walking back from church, my body swelled up with welts all over. By the time I got back to my residence, I was unable to breathe. The nuns there sent me to an allergist, where I learned that the condition I had could be fatal. If I were to suddenly jump into a cold lake, I would die. By this time, my physical problems did not phase me at all. My purpose was to suffer, and I became accustomed to it.

I had the freedom to stay with or leave this very intense program. I had seen sisters and priests come and then leave, not having completed the full three months. The sister who came the same day as I did left abruptly in the middle of the night.

I am the kind of person who says, "Okay, let's work on me." I was open to talking, to sharing. I did my homework diligently. I was asked to read books on creating boundaries, people pleasing, and even one on anger management. I was open to hearing what each counselor had to say. Sometimes I would come out of those sessions crying, cursing them under my breath, angry.

I was learning I can have feelings and it is okay to feel angry, sad, or afraid. It is what we do with those feelings. We can learn how to respond in a healthier way. It became clear to me I was a people pleaser. I also found that the more I investigated my childhood and my family, the more I realized my family is beautiful even with all its quirks.

One of my homework assignments was to talk to Sister Maria once a week. During one call, I was apologizing for an incident she had mentioned in her original evaluation. I had helped out a 15-year-old boy who was part of a gang, the Bloods. He reached out for prayers when the admiral of the gang was shot and killed on the street. As a sister I had helped him and his family, and through God's grace was able to get him out of the gang and moved to Harrisburg, Pennsylvania, to get help. Sister Maria was not pleased that I got too involved in helping him. My thought that a Blood member leaving a message on the answering machine, late one Friday night at the convent, asking for prayers because he had just witnessed his friend being shot, was a sign he wanted help. I was simply following my heart to help him.

Her response was, "It is not that anymore. It is what you did this past summer." She was referring to me discussing my situation with people outside the convent.

"Our community suffered so much, the way the friars and lay people treated us." Sister Maria did not realize that in the eyes of the friars and the lay people, what had happened to me over the past summer was the straw that broke the camel's back.

They had all seen the way previous sisters had been treated over the years and left. The community already had a bad reputation for casting out sisters. From the beginning, people outside the community had come to me and said there was something wrong. I always defended the sisters in the past, but now I was beginning to see that those people might be right.

After being in Michigan for four months, I had learned about myself. I met other sisters in the same boat. I went there as a "wilted flower," so down and depressed, but I was not put on any medication. Other sisters were diagnosed with a disorder and prescribed mood stabilizers or antidepressants.

At the end of the program, I was diagnosed as having a worldview influenced by my health problems that plagued me from infancy to the present. I knew this was true but had no idea how to heal from something so deep and fundamental. I had developed major insecurities and poor self-worth and I felt like everything bad always happened to me. By this time in my life, it had become the norm. I never would have thought that these feelings stemmed from these experiences. I was told spiritual healing in the heart was the answer.

In Michigan I received a mind healing. I decided to go back to the convent even after everything that transpired. The sisters agreed to take me back, probably out of guilt and a desire to make themselves look good. The professionals at the institute did not see any reason I could not live the life of a nun. They felt I could contribute a great deal to the community.

I came back to the Bronx in mid-January, with a renewed outlook, healthy coping skills, and a chance to participate in my religious community with love rather than fear. I continued my remote counseling on the phone by Sister Gabriel weekly for the next few months. Sister Teresa arranged this continued support, knowing the adjustment would be easier with help from those on the outside.

Years before, a young novice had been sent to that facility. They could not find anything wrong with her to prevent her from making vows. She had her issues, as we all do. A week after coming back, Sister Maria told the novice, "You have not changed. You must go."

The girl left soon after. When Sister Teresa heard this news, she was shocked. She claimed it was unhealthy of Sister Maria to not have patience and give her a chance. She wanted to ensure I continued to receive counseling by phone to support my new way of seeing things and a chance to implement what I had learned.

I had gotten help, but the rest of the community did not. The most important thing in cooperation is honesty, and I never received that from the sisters. It makes me crazy to think of all this and how unhealthy the community was when I was there. I admit I had my part in it—my reaction, my response to it all. But if you wrote down the facts of what was going on, and what was asked of me, any sane person would have seen how uncharitable it was.

When I returned, Sister Veronica, Sister Ignatius, and Sister Maria, each, in their own way, asked me how I was planning to make amends for my actions. Sister Ignatius told me the other sisters loved me. She claimed everything they had said, done, or not done had been out of love.

Isolating me, abandoning me, rejecting me. Is that love? During the time I was isolated at Hawthorne, an eminent bishop who was a close friend found out and he called me personally. He was incredibly surprised at how the community was treating me. Still, I suppose in their hearts they thought they did nothing wrong. Until this day not one has taken responsibility. They all blamed it on me.

Back in the Bronx once more, I was diligently working with the tools I learned at the facility. I shared with the friars and lay people that I was back and had a new mindset. They all said they saw a change in me.

As months went by, however, I found the fear and sorrow returning. I had been told it was a spiritual healing in the heart I needed. "How is that going to happen?" I asked, and was told, "Just pray. Only God can do it." At this point, it had nothing to do with the sisters anymore. It was between God and me.

I knew a friar who had had a parallel experience. After his time in Michigan, he went to Nebraska for a silent retreat. When he returned, he was a new man. He shared his experience with me. I told him about seeking spiritual healing, and he encouraged me to try the silent retreat as well.

Sister Maria gave me permission to go to Nebraska for one month. I wanted to believe it was her way of making amends, but I was still very naïve. She probably just wanted me away from the community. Of course, she would be in denial about her true motives.

I arrived in Nebraska with a Bible and a notebook. This retreat was for silent contemplation and journaling your thoughts and feelings. I was assigned a spiritual guide, Sister Immaculata. Each day she would give me at least seven scriptures to study. I wrote them out, asking the Lord Jesus what His will for me was. I trusted the Holy Spirit to guide me to an inner healing. She would visit once a day and would read aloud what I wrote in the last 24 hours. It was amazing to hear what I wrote. It was not me; it was God, Jesus, and the Holy Spirit writing through me.

Instead of a single month, I ended up staying over half a year. Through the grace of God, I was in silence for seven months and had a true spiritual healing. I felt like I'd had a St. Paul-type conversion—it was that radical! St. Paul was thrown from his horse and heard the voice of God. I was thrown off my emotional high horse, the one I had been riding on throughout my life.

I had perceived the sisters to be my enemies, but now I was finally internally free, a child of God, ready to go back to serve God and my sisters in the Bronx. At the beginning of March 2008, I returned home with a solid inner peace. I knew who I was in Christ. I was excited with my new light and life. I could not wait to share it with the community.

Of course, although I had changed profoundly, the sisters had not. Not one sister approached me with sincerity and asked about my months away. Never did I hear, "I missed you."

The community had grown, but the newer sisters were not even allowed to talk to me casually. I was only permitted to talk about my retreat experience once, at a gathering of the whole community of the different convents. I was assigned a specific time slot and given little freedom in what I could share.

Chapter 10

The bizarre experience began all over again. "You cannot do this. You cannot do that." My activities were restricted, and I felt I was being watched constantly. For instance, I was corrected after I spoke with one sister I was doing dishes with. I asked about her family and was told later that that was being intrusive. How sick is that?

I was transferred to the convent in Harlem. I was under the supervision of Sister Ignatius. She was a strange person. I will not go into that, except to say that when she was a novice, I took her to my cousin's house for the Fourth of July. They set off fireworks and put out a nice spread of food for us. It was fun. An entire month later, Sister Maria and I went for a walk. Sister Maria told me Sister Ignatius had been terribly uncomfortable at my cousin's house because fireworks are illegal. Sister Maria said it was poor judgment on my part to take her there. I was told not to do it again.

Incidents and stories such as this one showed me that they were like Pharisees—they held to the letter of the law, not the spirit. I always felt I could not be myself, a free-spirited person who loved God and wanted to give her whole life to Him and the community.

In August, I was talking to Fr. Koterski about what the sisters were doing, and how it was undermining my inner peace. Shortly afterwards, Sister Maria contacted me to meet with her. She stated, "I don't think you belong here anymore."

What could I say to that? I felt pressure as if I were pushed against the wall and there was no way out. I had done everything I could, and it was not what they wanted. That is when I finally stopped fighting and gave in to what she wanted. The decision was made for me to leave the religious life for good after I gave them my blood, sweat, and tears.

Of course, I did not know what to do next, and Sister Maria did not know the procedure since I was the first sister in final vows to leave this community. I had already arranged, weeks before, to go to Harrisburg for a two-week home visit the next day. She said, "Just go home, and I will find out what needs to be done." Then, as if it were the most natural thing in the world, we went out for pizza and ice cream.

Believe me, this decision was extremely painful for me to make. It was not on a peaceful note. It was bizarre. Sister Maria would be kind and nice but turn around and be cunning and baffling. That is what manipulation is. While I was in Harrisburg, neither Sister Maria nor Fr. Bonaventure called me even once to see how I was doing. I do not think they cared about me. I felt they had wanted me gone since two years prior, back in 2006, when they told me they needed a break. Of course, they would never admit that—it would not look good.

At this point, Irene, who had been so kind to me back in 2006, invited me to work and live at the home she had established for adult men and women with disabilities. Irene began this home so that when the time came, her son Sammy would have a loving place to live. It is a family setting. I took the offer, and I was grateful.

Irene and the Home were there for me when I needed love and support the most. I had been living a life of poverty, chastity, and obedience for almost twelve years. I had no money, wore a habit daily, and lived a simple life with nothing. If I went directly back into the secular world, I would have been lost. I was broken, crushed, and hurt. I needed a place of healing, and it was a good transitional place for me at the time.

Before I went back to the convent to say goodbye, turn in the car, and pick up my few possessions, Sister Maria called. She said I needed to write a letter stating my intention to leave the convent. She also asked me to write a letter to the friars stating it was my own free-will decision to leave the community. We both knew that was a lie.

When I asked Fr. Koterski what I should do, he said write the first letter but not the second. He told me, "When you say goodbye to her and the sisters on Tuesday, September 3, hand in your letter as well as your habit and say goodbye." He also advised me to meditate on the scripture, "Shake the dust off your feet (when you are not welcome)."

The day I left the convent had to be one of the hardest days of my life. It was like going to your own funeral. Irene was with me, to help me move. She heard me give a goodbye talk to the sisters. I do not know what I said. Irene said it was wonderful. Then I stood outside the chapel as each sister came out and said goodbye with a kiss on my cheek. Some were in tears. I felt like it was my open wake.

I went into the bathroom and changed into a long skirt and white top with a kerchief on my head. It just so happens the bathroom is on the same floor as the chapel, so I stepped inside for a moment. In the quiet it was just Jesus and me. I sat down, shook my feet in a symbolic gesture, and said, "This is for You." Then I left.

It was the hardest day, and yet it was Freedom Day. I was wounded and needed healing. I was told it was like a divorce, a time of grief. I kept asking, "Why, oh God, oh why?"

Chapter 11

Living at the home with adults with disabilities for two years was a gift. A time of grief, healing, letting go, learning to relate to people again. Fr. Koterski said my personality had been crushed by an unhealthy community. I did not know who I was when I left. The next day, I went to morning Mass dressed in a long skirt, white long-sleeved top, and a kerchief, trying to look like a sister. A parishioner after Mass came up to me and asked me what community I was from. I did not know what to say and I was totally crushed. Who was Sister Regina, and who was Gina?

I received an incredible amount of love from the adults with disabilities I served, and I submerged myself in it. I was taking care of them, and they were taking care of me.

During this time, Sister Maria tried to reach out by calling. It was too late for apologies. I found the courage to tell her I was angry at her and the sisters, and even the friars. None of the religious community were there for me when I needed them.

Nothing was ever done to address the sickness in that community. I felt alone, rejected by those who I thought were friends. I slowly lost touch with that life. The people and the events in New York dimmed as time healed my soul. I cried a lot and journaled. I waited for the sisters to confess what they did was wrong. I never heard a word of contrition and I expect I never will.

After living at and committing myself for two years to the Home, I felt it was time to move on. I was tired of serving and I discovered Gina's desire was to move by the beach and take a step away from service. I am grateful to those at the Home for allowing me the time to grieve and for the grace of restoration. For almost twenty years after Mom died, I had been on a journey seeking God. I went from one extreme to another, always serving others, rarely contemplating what I wanted from life.

I love God. I was surprised my faith sustained me through the trials of life before becoming a nun and after I was stripped of my vocation. I understand why people have chosen to leave the Catholic Church. I do not blame them. The path I chose—that is, to remain in the Church, keep the holy sacraments, and follow the commandments—was personal.

During my time in the community, I was blessed to meet Mother Teresa more than once. I traveled around the world—Italy, Germany, and France. I kissed the ring of Pope John Paul II before I entered the sisterhood. I also kissed Pope Benedict's ring as a sister. I have been to four world youth days, did a mission trip to Haiti, and met faithful, wonderful people.

I served the poor, the homeless, youth, the dying, even Bronx gang members. I know I have touched many people's lives. I am sure I have forgotten some events and people I have met as a sister. When I go to Heaven, I might glimpse how God has shown His love through me to my fellow man. Even through my suffering, I have felt God's love and know He has used me as an instrument of His peace.

Three years after I left the convent, I happened to be on a retreat for women. It was there I came to the realization that I was emotionally abused by the sisters. That awareness—and the deep acceptance that followed—helped free me from the trauma. I had been holding onto grudges and shame as well as making excuses for my abusers. When I finally claimed my pain, I felt okay. It was what it was.

I understand the feelings of those who have been sexually abused by the church. Shame, blame, and secrecy create confusion in your mind and soul when someone you trust hurts you. Betrayal feels more intense when someone who is supposed to love you uses that trust to take advantage. We look to the ministers of God's Word to be better than lay people. They may have a calling to do God's work, but some are unhealthy people that need help.

With my newfound acceptance, I separated myself from them. I could admit to myself and others when I was right or wrong. I chose, with God's grace, to forgive them all. It was an act of faith.

I asked for a sign from God that my forgiveness was genuine. Not long after, I got a message from Sister Maria asking for a callback. I had not spoken to her in a few years, so my instant thought was, *Oh my God, that is a sign. She is calling me to apologize!* My innocence allowed me to believe that things had changed.

The message was that a mutual friend, a former sister, had died. Sister Maria wanted to inform me of the funeral arrangements. We kept missing each other on the phone, but since I happened to be off on the day of the burial, I went to Staten Island for the funeral Mass. I got to the church early and saw Sister Maria and other sisters, but only from behind. We did not speak.

I knew I was on the road to healing because I did not feel any animosity. I didn't feel like I wanted to spit on them! I did speak to Fr. Mark, who at the time was the friars' community servant. He had been a good friend in the past. I felt hurt by him as well as the friars because nobody did anything to help, to stop the emotional abuse. I approached Fr. Mark after Mass and told him that I had forgiven him. His eyes opened wide, and he said, "What did I do?"

I answered, "I was emotionally abused by the sisters. Nobody was there for me during that time, or even after I left." I told him I was fine now, that I did not need him or the community anymore. He said he felt bad. He admitted it was a mess and he was sorry. He asked for my phone number to reconnect. I never heard from him.

I did not talk to any of the sisters after the Mass. They went straight to their cars to go to the cemetery. I was okay and felt a new peace in my heart. I noticed the church was on "Victory Boulevard," which I took as a sign from God that I was on the road of healing.

Three months later, I got another call from Sister Maria. Her message said, "Hi, Gina, this is Sister Maria. You looked great at Ann Lynn's funeral. I am calling to tell you to leave your address on my answering machine. I want to send you an invitation to the sisters' final vows."

When I heard that, I knew she was still sick and unhealthy, still trying to manipulate me. We had never spoken about the treatment I had received from the religious community. If I did call and go to the service, I would enable her behavior. The secret would be kept, and I would take the blame. Instead of calling, I wrote letters to both her and Fr. Bonaventure. I told them I knew I had been emotionally abused, and that I had finally forgiven them.

I was at peace writing and mailing them. I never heard a response. I am okay with their silence. It closed a chapter in my life. I was free and grateful to begin a new one.

Being a sister was part of my past. It is not who I am today. God is the only one who knows the suffering and pain I experienced during my time in the convent. Words do not convey my feelings, and I know God was with me as I persevered.

Writing those letters made me aware I had been hanging onto hope that somehow, I would be reunited with the community, even after years of proof they would not be there for me. I felt abandoned. That is where the hurt festered. I questioned God's plan for me when contemplating my experience. I have found peace with His plan for me. The support I wished to have received from the community is no longer a need. The help and support I have received from those who genuinely care for me has healed me on a very deep level.

I once heard, "You will only find five good friends in a lifetime. People who will be there for you, love you, and accept you, no matter what. It is hard to find them in one's lifetime."

Throughout my life, I have had friends—people who were there for a time, then left. We all have a journey, our own lives, our own paths, and it is in God's hands. With the eyes of Faith, I believe God puts people in our life for a time. Some remain. Some move on and are forgotten.

I went on a pilgrimage to Italy and Medjugorje twenty-one years ago, a year after my mom died, with Kelly, a former Franciscan sister. It was there the Blessed Mother took me under her mantle. I have good friends like Terry, a mother of eight children. I was like her ninth child. I took care of her brother with disabilities, who lived with me at the Home. Terry taught me the dos and don'ts of the world. I was lost being back in the real world. I also met my friend Patty after leaving the convent. She always encouraged me and gave me so much support. She does to this day!

Tom, I have known him for twenty years. He has been with me through the good and the bad. Peggy is a friend from Belmar. And there is Lori. I talk to her every day, sometimes two or three times a day. She has experienced grief in her lifetime. Tina, Kathie's sister-in-law, has been there for me many times. These are all friends who listen to me, love, and accept me.

Chapter 12

In October of 2010, two years after leaving the convent, I relocated to Belmar and took a winter rental on First Avenue. I was a block from the beach, which I loved. A dream come true to be by the ocean where I found peace and serenity. It was the first time I lived alone, and my first home since the convent and the Home. I moved in on October 14, which was a Friday. The following day, Saturday, I started a job bartending at McShays.

Where to live, where to work, and who to befriend was now completely my choice. After my mother died, I had been giving service to others for almost 18 years. I was tired of it. I needed a break. I had already come to terms with the fact that I had fulfilled one vocation in life as a religious sister and that door had closed. Moving to the beach opened the path to a new vocation for a single person.

I have always loved the beach, and now I was living close to one of the nicest beaches on the East Coast. I had bartended back in the day for four years, so I did not have a lot of choices about a career. It was either bartending or nunnery! I did not tell anyone that I used to be a Catholic nun. If it came up, I would say I was a social worker, or did missionary work in the Bronx. I wanted to be on my own, learn how to live life, and find a relationship. I did not know anyone in the Belmar area, so bartending was my social life and my way of meeting new people.

I had not worked at McShay's for a month when Danny walked in one Sunday afternoon. Later, he explained that he never went there because it was too expensive. He did not know why he walked in that day. When he saw me behind the bar, a petite young lady with a beautiful smile, he believed it was God who brought him in there.

It was God who brought our lives and our paths together. He said I was kind to him, with a great big smile, treating him like he was the only person in the room. I interacted with all my customers like that, but Danny felt I gave him special treatment. He told me later he fell in love with me the moment he laid eyes on me. In one of his letters he wrote, "I might have fallen in love with you before we met." It was my smile, my kindness—not to mention my sexy butt that he noticed as I walked away from him after I served him a bottle of Coors Light.

I do remember him walking in the bar that day. I thought he was quite handsome. We got to talking, and he shared with me how he was a retired police officer and had grown up in the neighborhood. That day was the third anniversary of his retirement. I thought he was kind, personable, and attractive. We chit-chatted about everything. Our mutual love of playing pool was shared. There was something about him that I liked right away, but I also told him I was not going to date anyone. He told me later that when he first saw me, he said to himself, "This is a woman I am going to date."

The next day, Monday, I was off. I went to the Boathouse to meet up with my friend Julie to shoot pool. Who happened to be there but Danny? He was with a lady, sitting at the bar. I did not think anything of it. We just waved, but he came over to the pool room to say hello and watch. He could not believe I had remembered his name!

Danny would come into McShays just to sit and talk, and of course have a couple of Coors Light bottles. He asked me out many times. I kept saying no. He told me to ask the owner what a good guy he was. Everyone knew Danny Franklin, a.k.a. "Danny the Kid." They all had good things to say, so instead of making a real date, I said, "Let's meet at PKs to shoot pool Thursday night at 9:00 PM."

Thursday, he stopped by the bar in the afternoon. He had to go to a wake with his mom and promised he would be back before 9:00 PM. I wanted to opt out. I suggested we cancel and go another time. He said not to worry; he would be back. That night after work, we met at PK's. We shot pool. I had fun. I shot well and beat him. (He claimed he let me win.)

Danny confessed he was distracted just watching me in my tight black jeans with a pink snug top and black clogs. He always remembered what I wore. I did too—it was more a lavender top, but it *was* snug! When the night was over, he walked me to my car, kissed me on the cheek, and said he had had a good night. I told him, "Me, too." I remember being surprised and impressed that it was only a kiss on the cheek.

We talked often on the phone, and he would visit me at work. We would go out after my shift, usually to a bar. One Monday when I was off, I went to his mom's house where he was living in Lake Como. He was working outside of the house. I asked him if he wanted to go out to dinner and then to the movies. He said, "Of course," and so that night I picked him up. I met his mom, whom everybody called Jane. Eventually, I would call her "Mom." That evening was our first real date.

We went to TGI Friday's, then to the movies to see Robert Downey Jr. in *Due Date*. That first night, our conversation was all about me being a social worker in the South Bronx, serving the gang members and the homeless. I even shared with him about that murder case I was involved with in 1996. He spoke more extensively about being a police officer—deep things—and was honest about his former marriage and love for his kids.

After the movies, we went to the boardwalk in Belmar and just walked a while. When he took my hand, my first crazy thought was, *This is a man who would clean my butt if I was sick.* I cannot explain it. I just knew it.

That night, in my car, about to drive to my apartment, I whispered to the Lord, "I would love for Danny to be my best friend." The moment I said that Danny came running out of his house, made me open my car window, and blurted out, "I want to be your best friend." I almost died from the shock of coincidence.

We became best friends. We told each other everything, or almost everything. At first, I did not feel comfortable telling him I had been a Catholic nun. I was cautious. I did not want to scare him. I had learned my lesson. In the past, when I would meet guys in the bar, or on a train, or elsewhere, I'd tell them all about my experiences as a nun. They would never call me to go out. I asked my friend Terry why. She told me "Do not...I repeat, do

NOT tell a guy you are an ex-nun. Just smile and say you were a social worker."

My conviction in Danny's gentle nature never changed even as the dynamics of our relationship did. He was a gentleman, always opening the door to the car, to the house, wherever we would go. He would grab my hand affectionately and speak lovingly. One week after we met, I was on the phone with Terry, telling her about Danny. I admitted I was beginning to have feelings for him. I told her he treated me like a lady. I asked, "Should I tell him I was a nun?"

"Yes, now you should. Either he will run, or he will stay."

As soon as I got off the phone with her, my phone rang. It was Danny, and he said, "I need to talk to you." I asked him where he was, and he said, "Out in front of your apartment."

I laughed. "Are you stalking me?"

"No, can you come down, or can I come up?" I told him I would come down. I approached him and kissed him on the cheek. He asked, "What are you not telling me about yourself?"

My mouth dropped open. I felt like it was a sign from God, from the Holy Spirit. I explained, "I was a Catholic nun for twelve years."

He paused, then said, "Okay. You are still coming for dinner, right?" It did not scare him away. I was glad. I did not understand my feelings, and I was falling for him. *Could it be because he was my first date after the convent? A guy who took an interest in me, respected and listened to me—all the things I did not get while I was there?*

I see now how God put two broken hearts together to love each other for who we were. But people are not defined solely by our mistakes. We were children of God that found each other. Our love was truly magical. I believe it came from God. I believed now and I still do.

I had been through a lot. I found tremendous healing through Danny's love. We had fun and complemented each other. The only obstacle that got in our way was the disease of alcoholism. Danny drank daily.

Chapter 13

I found out Danny was an alcoholic weeks after I met him. The day before Thanksgiving 2010, he had a seizure in his mother's kitchen. I was there but did not comprehend what was going on. Mom was yelling at him, "You are a drunk!"

I did not know what to do, and I did not understand what an alcoholic was. I thought they were people who drank a lot but could easily stop. It had not scared Danny to learn I was once a nun; he stayed. That night I stayed in the kitchen. It did not scare me because I did not know about alcoholism yet.

I was not raised in an alcoholic or addiction-ridden family. We had our problems, but nothing major. I drank in college, and by the end of the four years, my friends thought I was an alcoholic, but I stopped once I moved back with my parents. I thought it would be easy for Danny to quit, too. I said, "Just don't drink, and I will stay." He tried, and I stayed. Sometimes he succeeded, sometimes he went back to it, but I was falling in love with him, so I stayed even as he drank.

I expressed my love for him and encouraged him to stay sober. I wanted to spend the rest of my life with him as husband and wife. We both knew the depth of our love. God knew the desire in our hearts. We wanted to live a simple life as a happily married couple. Alcoholism was a dark force not about to let that happen.

Danny had a pension. He planned to keep working as a carpenter. He loved carpentry and was skilled in the trade. As he worked on a project, he would talk to himself. His mom, Jane, testified to that habit. He was a perfectionist, always cleaning up after himself. He loved what he did.

We dreamed of buying a run-down house, and he would fix it up. Danny was a planner. He knew I was simple, not materialistic.

He described how nice our home would be and consulted me on details. He insisted it would be our house. We loved to communicate. We talked all the time. He loved that as much as I did.

Our favorite TV show was *Golden Girls*, and when he was in the room he would look into my eyes and sing the theme song. He knew it by heart and constantly would tell me, "Thank you for being a friend."

I feel blessed to have experienced a love where I was someone's dream girl. He was a man that every girl dreams of being loved by. Someone who loves you and accepts you for who you are.

We talked endlessly about spending the rest of our lives together as husband and wife. We would share our dreams, our hopes, our future when we walked the boardwalk. It was one of our favorite things to do. We didn't do it for exercise. Instead, it was slow, romantic, hand in hand, and every few blocks we would stop by a bench or railing overlooking the beach and slowly, sensually kiss.

It was just him and me as if no one else existed. Danny joked about how it would be when we were in our eighties. He described us walking the boardwalk hand in hand, bald, toothless, with canes or walkers. Everyone who passed the aged couple would marvel at the love we still had. People would just know how we loved each other.

It was so natural to be with him. We enjoyed our time together and missed each other when apart. The only arguments we had were over his drinking. I knew there was a problem and I thought I had the solution. Do not drink, and we will live happily ever after.

Early in our relationship I told him, "I love you, but I cannot put up with the drinking." I was so uneducated about alcoholism. I really thought a person could stop because I asked him to. He loved me and knew I did not like him drinking. I felt that should be enough motivation for him to stop.

I knew it was wrong for an alcoholic to continue to drink. I had no concept of AA and Al-Anon. When I told him he needed to get help, he promised, "I'll call a counselor I know that helped me before." He started to see her, and I went, too. She told me about Al-Anon, a support group for family and friends whose lives are affected by someone else's drinking, and Danny encouraged me to go so I could learn more about him and the disease.

Walking through the doors of Al-Anon, many would say, is the first step as well as the hardest. When I walked in, I thought it was all about Danny, "my" alcoholic. I thought they would show me how I could stop him from drinking. What could I do or not do? What could I say or not say to help him?

It did not take long to learn what Al-Anon was about: changing my own behaviors and attitudes!

There are twelve steps in Al-Anon, similar to any twelve-step program. It's a spiritual program. The steps are there to help each individual member to find peace and serenity, whether or not they are living with an alcoholic. What one learns in an Al-Anon meeting is that alcoholism is a family disease, all are affected, and that we have no control over alcoholics. When I first heard these steps, I had a sense of pride. I knew all this from my time as a Catholic nun. I already knew there was a Power greater than me, God. I gave my life and my will over to God every day, in my sisterhood. Every night the community would do a moral inventory. We called it examining our conscience. We discussed how to make amends and practice forgiveness.

To be humble, to reach out, especially to have a conscious contact with God—that is what we called the present moment. I felt I was ahead of the game in the Al-Anon meetings. I knew it all. *This will be easy.* Al-Anon gave me hope for myself and for Danny.

Al-Anon is a safe place to share your strength, hope, and experience. I heard other men and women living with alcoholics share how once they realized and accepted they were powerless over the alcoholic and started taking care of themselves, let go, and let God do His work, their alcoholic loved ones found recovery. I thought if it could happen to them, it would be possible for us to receive the gifts of serenity and sobriety. The message filled me with hope.

I was a beginner back then, and I am still learning today. I listened to stories of adult children who grew up in alcoholic families. I empathized with their fears and insecurities. I was sympathetic to those who had suffered abuse from their mothers, fathers, or other family members. I heard the lies, the secrets, the manipulation, and craziness—which seemed normal to them.

I came to realize two things: One, I was blessed with a healthy and loving family. Two, I had experienced the same kind of dysfunctional behavior as a sister in a religious order! The similarities were eye opening. In hindsight, I felt those same feelings in the convent, granted the sisters were not actually drinking like alcoholics did.

I thank God for Danny, for the experience of loving an alcoholic. He was a child of God. A wonderful, loving, gracious man who suffered from the disease of alcoholism. Danny sober was everything I wanted in a man: affectionate, sensitive, loving, and humorous.

For those who do not understand the disease of alcoholism, alcoholics are seen as weak. People assume they could stop if they really wanted to. Their behavior is perceived as self-destructive and unmanageable by choice. They see the influence of alcohol and not the man or woman who is powerless over the substance.

I was able to see Danny for the man he wished he could be. We both knew God brought us together. We had a story to tell, a message to be heard. That is my goal—to reach out to other alcoholic families and friends and assure them there is love beyond the disease.

There is so much more I could write about Danny. I think of him often, especially when I see butterflies. I remember the way he gazed at me and recall his left-sided wink with affection. When he ate his favorite ice cream—chocolate—watching TV, I would look at him, thinking how I loved him. He would stop and look at me and wink. No words can describe the thrill it gave me.

Danny, sober and in recovery, was intelligent, witty, and observant. These qualities served him well as a police officer. We yearned to live a simple life. We had arguments and knew life would present us with problems, but we were a team and had each other's backs. We just wanted to be a typical husband and wife.

When Danny was sober, he was a wonderful man, everything I desired. I knew he was an alcoholic, but I accepted that. The alcoholic was not who I saw and knew. I learned to separate the disease from the person. He was a person, a man—my man. I believed in him. I encouraged him. His mother and I were his biggest fans.

Not only did I believe in him; I believed in God, who I perceived as Danny's Higher Power. I knew God can and will do anything to help those who believe and even those who do not. Danny gave me a ring with a cross and the words "With God All Things Are Possible" engraved. I believed in His Word. Since God did not answer my prayers with Mom and being in the convent, I surely believed He would answer my prayers for Danny.

As I write down these memories of Danny and who he was, it saddens me. I know alcoholism is a disease. I know alcohol abuse was a catalyst to his death. I know it was not what he wanted. I know the shell of a man he became before he died was not him.

He hated his addiction as much as I did. He wanted to stop. He wanted to give me a life of sobriety, recovery—a great life. He knew the pain and hurt that I endured from the disease. I know he was sorry, but that is the cunning, baffling part. It is a disease of lies. Alcoholism is a brain disease. So many people are not aware of this. So many have died from it.

Danny hated what alcohol did to him. The lies compounded, kept piling up, lies that had to be told to support the lies from before. Dishonesty destroys relationships. The sickness affects everyone who interacts with alcoholics—family, friends, neighbors, co-workers, and the public. Danny was sick. I became sick. I had crazy thoughts and overreactions. I manipulated, denied, and threatened.

I was not helping Danny. I was an enabler trying to control him. If anything, I was making things worse. I learned I did not cause his alcoholism, I could not cure it, nor could I control it. Those are the three "C's" of Al-Anon. There is also a fourth—how do we learn to *cope* with it?

Danny and I both tried and tried working the program. It is a lifelong process. A lifestyle we both wanted, to live sober and free. Danny tried four different rehabs in a short amount of time. He had periods of sobriety but kept going back to the bottle. I do not know why. There are those who will say it has to do with free will, but I know how sick Danny was. He really did not have a choice.

A whole new thing for me was to try and understand where God fit into this mix. God can intervene. God can create miracles. Why, oh why, was Danny one of the ones who did not make it? Why did this happen to me?

Chapter 14

In May of 2012, it was Danny's choice to go out to New Solution, a rehab in Phoenix, Arizona. In the two months he was there, he finally found a sobriety with which he could live. We talked every day by phone, and I told him I would be waiting for him at home. He was doing well, working the program, and loved being out there. He had made many friends and had even found the kind of job he had always wanted, where he could use his skills as a carpenter. He was so excited, but he wanted his truck and tools.

New Solution gave him permission to fly back to New Jersey to pick them up and to drive the truck back to Arizona. Danny came home from Arizona on July 12, 2012. When I first saw him coming in the front door, I fell in love with him all over again, or even more in love.

Danny would always say, "I don't know if I can fall more in love with you." I understood what he meant when I saw him. His children were there, so I stepped aside to let them embrace him first. I knew he was all mine. I was going to be with him all night, and even for the rest of my life. Still, I had to hold myself back from attacking him!

We had a nice dinner that night. Mom was happy. After dinner I helped Danny pack, filling one suitcase after another with clothes, important papers, and necessities. At one point, with that twinkle in his eyes, he said, "Gee, I do not think I will ever come back here again. Only to visit."

He had found work, a place to live, and most important of all, good, solid sobriety in Arizona. I encouraged, "Get established out there in your recovery, and I will come there. I will support your recovery even if it's in Timbuktu." It did not matter where; it mattered how. Living a sober life together was what we both wanted.

That night he took time to make amends with me. Of course, I forgave him. I loved him so much. I knew the real Danny. I am a person who easily forgives, or else I just let it go. He knew things he did were wrong. I was wrong too in some ways. But our love was beyond it all. We were ready to begin again.

I got to experience the sober Danny that night. The next morning, before I went to work, I embraced Danny and his mom. They were leaving that morning for Arizona. Mom was at peace and incredibly happy that Danny was sober. She was going to help him begin a new life in Arizona. I said a prayer with them—we always prayed together like that. I blessed his truck with holy water and put a rosary in it, knowing and believing they would drive safely. I left for work feeling happy and full of hope.

Later that day, he called me from the road as they were filling up with gas. The trip had been going well. That night, around 8:45 PM, I called Danny's cell phone. Mom picked up and said Danny was driving so I could not talk to him right then. Mom said, "Everything is going so peacefully. Keep praying."

I said, "Tell Danny I love him. I love you too, Mom. Talk to you both tomorrow." That was the last time I spoke to Mom, the last time I ever heard her voice.

I stayed at Mom's house to watch the dogs for the weekend. Mom was scheduled to fly back Monday from Arizona. Saturday, July 14, at 6:30 AM, the house phone rang. I answered it, still half-asleep. It was Danny's sister from Texas. She was terribly upset. She told me Mom and Danny had been in a serious accident with the truck. "Mommy went home and is with Poppy, and Danny is severely burned and is in a hospital in Indianapolis." That was all she knew.

I was in shock. My insides just froze. I started to cry. I could not believe what had happened. It seemed so surreal, but it was true. I reached out to friends, asking for prayers, just crying and crying. The same thought ran through my mind repeatedly: *How could this be?* Nobody could tell me what was going on with Danny.

We were told by a state trooper Danny had been driving the truck headed west on Route 70 at about 1:30 AM in Clay County.

He suddenly swerved to avoid hitting a deer and lost control. The truck went off the road onto the median. It hit one tree after another until finally hitting a big tree. The truck caught fire on Mom's side. A passing truck driver saw the fire and stopped to help. He got Danny out by cutting the seat belt.

Danny was on fire. The truck driver threw him down to roll in the dirt. They could not get to Mom because she was already engulfed in flames. She was consumed by the fire. This memory is painful even after so much time has passed.

Danny told me he was conscious the whole time. He knew Mom died on impact and helplessly watched her burn. Danny tried to get out, but he was pinned to the wheel and burning up. He said he was fighting to get out. He got to a point where he was praying for God to take him, and that is when he was rescued. I cannot imagine what he went through, what he saw and felt. Through all this trauma, he was conscious and sober.

That day, friends came by to keep me company. My friend Lori picked me up to go to the 5:00 PM mass. News of Danny's condition was minimal. His older sister was in touch with the hospital. She was flying out on Sunday to see what was going on. After Mass we went to the Shrimp Box for dinner. I had no appetite but was told to eat for strength.

I looked at my cell phone and saw I had gotten a message from Danny. I was excited to hear his raspy voice, anxious to call him back. When I did, the first thing he said was, "Mom is dead. She saw me sober." He was heavily sedated. He was deeply burned, over 35 percent of the right side of his body, from his head to his ankle, right to the bone. He was in incredible pain. He saw himself as a burnt rump roast. I was told burns are the worst trauma.

I repeatedly told him, "I love you." I assured him he was going to survive this, sending as much encouragement and love as I could over the phone. I felt so helpless.

As soon as I could, I packed up my life in Jersey. I went to Indianapolis to be with Danny while he recovered from his injuries. After his release from the hospital, the local AAs opened their hearts and homes to us. We did not know anyone. We stayed with a couple, Jim and Brenda, for a few weeks. Each of them had 25 years of sobriety. They were very kind and generous. Alcoholics reaching out to another alcoholic in need. That's what we experience and how the AA program works. In September we got a place together and became engaged at a beautiful sober gathering in the backyard of Jim and Brenda's house. Danny celebrated 90 days as well. As Danny continued to heal from his injuries, we began to make wedding plans for April of 2013.

It was not long before Danny began drinking again. It's easy to see why any person, alcoholic or not, would drink to ease the physical, mental, and emotional pain from an event like the one he experienced. He plunged deep into his addiction. No doubt he was suffering from the memory of the accident and the loss of his mother. I was trying to protect myself and do the right thing based on what I learned in Al-Anon. In October of 2012, I kicked him out and made him find his own place to live.

While he was drinking, I kept my distance. Our communication was limited. I practiced "tough love." I relapsed from working on my program. I criticized him, reviled him with anger. I cried, I yelled, and I begged. I could not see his suffering because all I could feel was my own pain. It never dawned on me how much he suffered emotionally and physically from the accident.

I focused on his drinking. I thought if "detaching with love" worked to get other Al-Anons' loved ones sober, it would work for Danny. I even blocked his number in the last days of his life. I thought I was doing the right thing. I still loved him, still believed that he would find recovery and that God would help him.

It was Holly, a lady I did not know, who came to me and said that she had not seen Danny in days. So that is why I went to his place on March 20, banging on his door with Holly. Then we called the police. It took a while for them to open the door. They were arguing with me since I was not on the lease and was not a blood relation. I noticed this lady Holly, an older woman, was talking about Danny like she knew him well.

When the police officers found him dead and told me, I broke down. He was fifty-three years old. I wanted to see him, but they advised me not to. They would not let me into the apartment. I saw him in the body bag as they carried him out. I wanted to run to him, but they held me back. I needed to touch him one last time. In shock, confused, floating in a surreal reality, I was there in body but out of my mind. Everything became cloudy.

Holly tried to console me as the police made calls to Danny's family. Dazed, I called Jim and Brenda, the couple from AA that had taken us in after the crash. They happened to be in the neighborhood and came to the apartment complex to comfort and support me.

I waited with Jim and Brenda as Danny's body was removed. The cause of death was apparent: he had fallen and hit his head. He died from the disease of alcoholism. The condition of his body led them to believe he had been dead for days. I was a wreck. I plunged into my own familiar dark place—feelings of fear, sadness, self-pity, and brokenness. *Why me? Why Danny? Why us?* Jim and Brenda insisted I come home with them.

Since I was only Danny's fiancée, I had no legal rights. His daughter, who was 22 years old at the time, had all the legal rights. She eventually gave me access to his apartment. Once I got that, I went to his place by myself.

It was one of the hardest things I ever had to do. There was blood from his head on the kitchen floor as well as fluid from the decaying body. I found so many empty beer cans scattered around. I did not see any full cans, not even in the refrigerator. I assumed he was detoxing, fell, and hit his head. I kept telling myself that story and anyone who wanted to know what happened. I thought it would keep him from looking like a bad person.

The beer was not the worst. Cleaning up his bathroom, I found used condoms in the garbage. Shock, anger, and shame raged through me. Here I was telling everyone what a wonderful guy he was and how I was going to marry him. This was how I found out he had been unfaithful to me. I went through his phone and saw Holly's phone calls and texts.

Holly looked old to me. I could not see Danny being attracted to her. I called her and accused, "Did you fuck my Danny boy?"

She was speechless and then finally admitted, "We were lonely." She assured me that Danny loved me through it all, which I did know.

Boy, did we have a feud of texting back and forth. I named her the bar whore, never using her name. Few people know about this part of my story. I was so ashamed, so hurt, I kept it to myself. I never wanted anyone to know. I knew it would look bad. I remember Danny's promise he made to me when he was sober. After the accident he promised me that he would never die drinking or be unfaithful to me, but that is exactly what happened. Add more pain to the wound, Danny had so much respect for me that we would wait for our wedding night to consummate our love.

After Danny's death, my smile went away entirely. My discoveries in the apartment plunged me into a state of depression that went way beyond grief. After Danny's death, I just kept sliding deeper and deeper into my pain and self-hatred. I felt like a zombie. In my darkest hours I began to hate God. I felt deceived and abandoned by the man I was to marry and the Higher Power I had once been married to.

April 20, 2013, was to have been mine and Danny's wedding day. We had reserved a time for our ceremony at St. Roch's church in Indianapolis. Since we already reserved time, I decided to hold a memorial service for him on that day. Instead of walking down the aisle in a white dress with a smile on my face, I walked that aisle wearing black, with a broken heart and in tears.

Many friends came from AA as well as Al-Anon to support me and to say farewell to Danny's memory. He had already been interred in New Jersey by that time—his ex-wife had overseen everything. I was only the fiancée; I had no legal authority. However, in an act of kindness, she later gave me a little bit of his ashes and put it in a cross necklace for me to wear.

I organized the memorial service with help from friends in Indianapolis. I had a program with pictures of Danny, and the two of us. After the memorial Mass, food was served in the hall that we had reserved for our wedding reception. We did not need that big of a hall. Tables overflowed with flowers and food, softly lit by candles. I know it would have been beautiful because I had planned the event in a state of happiness. I really do not remember how it looked or what transpired at the memorial. I was going through the motions, but I felt incredibly sad and alone and simply existed.

I had dreamed of a wedding wearing a white gown, dancing with the love of my life to our wedding song, "Can't Help Falling in Love with You" by Elvis Presley. My gown hung in the closet, covered in plastic, never worn. My empty arms would never again hold the man I loved, and as I heard the music in my head, all I felt was numb.

I eventually brought my unworn wedding gown back with me to the Jersey Shore. I kept it in my closet for years, unable to part with the dream that had become a nightmare. I finally donated the gown to a thrift store. I hope whoever purchased it had a good day and life with the man she loved.

Chapter 15

I went to my sister Kathie's and her husband Kenny's place at Kueka Lake in July of 2013 to rest and try to heal after Danny's death. I poured my soul out into my journal, writing every day by the soothing waters of the lake. My heart ached, and I wrote. My pain swelled, and I sobbed.

I lived in confusion. *How could God have allowed this to happen?* I would not speak my thoughts aloud for fear of backlash. My family, my friends, and most Christian people I know would argue God did not do this to me. I carefully phrased my words, "How could God *allow* this to happen?" Deep down, I felt and believed that God was responsible.

Here is a part of what I wrote at the time:

I feel it's okay to feel, to think, even to say that, because for me it goes to my core, and it's how I feel at this moment of time. Yes, I blame God, saying that, writing that and thinking it's real to me, it's who I am right now in my situation. I am tired, not only physically but mentally and emotionally. If you look back and write out all the things that have happened in my life, a lot of it, most of it is tragedy. In those times of pain and suffering I would just smile and take it all. I'd rather see myself in pain and suffering than my family and friends, or even other people.

I stayed at Kueka Lake until the second week in August. The last day I was there, August 13, 2013, I wrote:

There are days I am filled with anger: at Danny, at God, at myself, in how it all happened. You see, with alcoholism, other "isms" come with it like lying, cheating, manipulation. The alcoholic, when drinking, becomes a totally different person. *They become self-centered. Sad to say, they think of themselves all surrounded by pain and depression, and their only way out is drinking. It's a brain disease, I'm told. It's a disease and a sickness that they have. The drinking Danny was not the Danny I know and love. There is no cure in this lifetime. The only way is a spiritual way through the grace of God.*

Now I question God, and I'm so angry. Why did He allow this to happen? He could have intervened in the accident. Danny was doing the right thing. Keeping him alive as well as conscious through the whole thing—was that necessary?

Look what God did for all those people who have years of sobriety. Each one would say it was an act of God, Divine intervention when they look back and see where they were and where they are today. So where was that intervention for my Danny?

During that time in New Jersey when we were going to AA meetings, I would hear at the beginning that it is a simple program but there are those that are incapable of grasping it. It isn't their fault; they're simply born that way. I thought then "I hope that's not Danny. Danny has a lot to offer." All alcoholics do. You know it's a disease when you see the true person beyond it.

I just spoke to a friend, Freddy, from my past as a sister. I hadn't spoken to him in years, but for some reason— God?—I called him and shared my pain. He felt my pain and was familiar with the disease of alcoholism. Freddy is one of a kind, a unique thinker. He said to me, "You know, Gina, God does not punish alcoholics for being an alcoholic. No, He called Danny home to be with Him. It was his time." So true, yet hard to grasp.

My faith is being challenged, big time. I have taken a rest from church, praying, meditation, reading the scriptures, reading Al-Anon literature, even from working the Steps. I am tired of being me, with everything I have endured. I have been healed, reconciled with Mom's death as well as the sisters with this time of my life, and with what has happened I am broken and in deep grief. Right now, God is on the couch.

You see, during my time with the sisters I was going towards God, begging for Him, searching for Him. But now my prayer is tears, grief. We have a love-hate relationship. I know that through this pain He is there somewhere, and I do know that He loves me and accepts me for where I am at. So I am still on a journey of grief, tears, pain, recovery, just taking it one day at a time.

I do realize the greatest pain of all is that I miss my Danny boy very, very much. I love him so much. It's the bottom line of it all: I miss him. He will always be the love of my life, my babe, my Danny boy. And I know through everything that I am the true love of his life.

We were both seeking throughout our lives and found each other and loved and healed each other. A love, I'm told, only few will experience in this life. Even many married couples who don't live with the disease will never know the love Danny and I have. Now our love will go deeper, and in a different way. It's a journey that is not of my own. I don't know how my life will end. At this time, it's a story in itself. Now I am leaving the lake, it's going to be a painful road ahead. I don't know how, when or where but I will get through it all.

After leaving Kueka Lake, I reluctantly returned to Indianapolis to pack up my belongings. There were too many unhappy memories. At this point I was living with a Christian woman who heard my tragic story. She did not know me yet, but she invited me to stay with her until I had decided to return to New Jersey and try to rebuild my life.

I worked at the Steak 'n Shake restaurant for a brief time while in Indianapolis. The manager, Kristen, was a kind and supportive friend. In September of 2013, her husband, Charles, a quiet, respectful man whom I had not yet met, drove me all the way back to Jersey Shore in a U-Haul with my red 1994 Pontiac Sunbird towed behind it. Charles drove the whole way to New Jersey in 13 hours, unloaded my belongings into a storage unit, and stayed at the Belmar Lodge overnight. It was his very first time seeing the beach! He flew home the next day. He was a quiet man. Even though he did not know me at all, he went out of his way to help me because, at the time, I had no one. The people in the Indianapolis area are very friendly—true Christians and die-hard Colts fans. I look back and see how God sent many angels to help me when I was at a dark place of grieving.

When I returned to Jersey Shore, I felt very much alone. My home with Danny and his mom was gone as if it had burned to the ground with them in the accident. I was one of the walking dead. I clung to a dream that when I came back to the Jersey Shore, I would find him and Mom again—my family, my home. I would wake up and find it was all a terrible nightmare. Driving by the house on Bradley Terrace, behind Mary's Pub, I found myself feeling so empty, so sad, so depressed. *Am I never going to have a home like that again?*

Mary, an elderly lady I knew from my New Jersey Al-Anon meetings, offered me a room in her house in Belmar. She was a widow whose alcoholic husband was 20 years sober before he died. Mary was a stern, crotchety old Irish lady. She said what she meant, meant what she said, and tended to say it meanly. I needed a place to stay and was grateful for her offer.

I had a bedroom in Mary's house. She made dinner every night, and the air filled with stories of her life with an alcoholic. She talked. I listened. Mary did not hold back sharing her suffering, and she gave equal importance to joy. After her husband got sober, they enjoyed traveling together. Those who did not know Mary well thought she was an unhappy person. I witnessed another side of her. She certainly told it like it was...the good and the bad.

A friend helped me get a server job at Perkins Pancake House. I worked with a woman, Michelle, who was kind and loving. She had lost her husband, and she understood my pain and grief. My Danny had died of alcoholism. It was a stigma which caused extra pain when I shared. Non-program people do not have an understanding or sympathy for death under those circumstances. It is a slow suicide.

I was still in more pain. My face was etched with sadness. I went back to Al-Anon and shared my grief, my loss of Danny. I felt like nobody understood. I was frustrated when I heard people in meetings complaining that their sober loved ones did not do the dishes, or that the drinking ones forgot to take out the trash. I kept thinking, *You should thank God they're still alive!* Rarely did anyone approach me. I needed comfort or words of sympathy. I was hurt, angry, and looked for consolation and love.

The more I went to Al-Anon, the more disenchanted I became. I hated hearing about alcoholics "not wanting it." When I would share that Danny wanted the AA program, he simply could not *get* it, they dismissed him as a "lost cause."

I am convinced that Danny died on March 17, 2013. Whenever St Patrick's Day rolls around, I am reminded of what the police told me when they found him. According to the coroner's report, although he was found dead on March 20, he had been dead for a few days. They could not pinpoint exactly when—it is not like you see on *Law and Order*, where they can tell the time and date of a person's death so precisely.

I did my own investigation. I looked at his cell phone, and the last call was to his voicemail on Saturday, March 16 at 11:45 PM. There were no outgoing calls after that. Danny would always call me, even when we were living apart, and when I did not hear from him for those following days, I thought he was getting the help he needed.

I stayed away. It was Al-Anon advice, to detach with love. I felt bad that I did not listen to my heart. On March 16, I went to a 5:00 PM Mass at St. Rocco's. It was my MO, begging God to heal Danny. I would always drive by Danny's complex afterwards and look for his Bronco. When I left Mass that night on my way home, something inside me said to call Danny and see if he wanted me to get a pizza. Then I heard the voice of Al-Anon saying, "Do not go. Let him be. Stay away." So that is what I did.

When I found him on the 20th, seeing his last call was Saturday night, I felt so guilty and upset with Al-Anon. I went through the "what ifs." *What if I had called him? What if I had stopped with a pizza? What if I had listened to my heart instead of Al-Anon suggestions?* I felt guilty for an exceedingly long time, because if we had never met in McShays and I had not insisted on his getting help for his alcoholism, he and his mom might still be alive. If our paths never crossed, who knows where they would have been? The compulsive analysis added intense pain and heaviness to my mind, heart, and soul.

I was pissed. I grieved deeply for Danny. I was to hold onto my suffering for years. It was a way to keep his memory alive. It was hard for me to mention his name. When it came to the first holidays, I would not and could not say happy or merry *anything!* My grief was all consuming, written on my face. I wore it like shattered glass. My grief cut me with every movement and kept others away, fearful of my fragility.

Christmas time of 2013, I went out to dinner with another Al-Anon friend, Peggy—something I rarely did. I forgot to call Mary. When I got home that night, all my belongings were packed up on my bed. She was kicking me out because I did not call her to tell her I would not be home for dinner that evening. All I kept thinking: *Why is all this happening to me?*

In shock, I called Peggy, who lived about seven blocks away. I told her I had been kicked out. She and her husband Chris welcomed me. They had a room in the basement that I partially moved into. I was lost, living out of my 1992 red Pontiac, as well as the basement room. Tears were my best friend. They were constant.

Although people were trying to be kind, living with others temporarily was not working for me. I was just getting tired of moving from one place to another. I felt like a nomad. It motivated me to find a place of my own. I found an apartment I could just afford on my salary—a one-year lease in Oxford Apartments in Neptune City.

Finding that apartment was another time God was watching out for me. When I was still living with Mary and working at Perkins, I was stopped by a Neptune City police officer while driving my red Pontiac Sunbird. He claimed I had been on my cell phone while driving and gave me a ticket. No amount of explanation, or tears, could persuade him to let me off. I was angry. I had not been on my cell. I had been crying. I had a red car, and Danny warned me that police officers loved to stop pretty girls driving red cars. At the time I felt anything but pretty.

I was homeless, driving around, looking for an apartment, when a Mercedes Benz rear-ended me. An elderly woman got out of the driver's seat. She was very apologetic. Instead of calling the police, she said she wanted to compensate me for the damage and handed me some bills. Then she took off. Thinking I could now afford a tankful of gas, I eagerly counted the bills in my hand. Imagine my dismay when I found only $4.00!

That same day I got stopped again—by the same police officer as last time! He said I had something hanging from my rear-view mirror. Half the cars in New Jersey have things hanging from their mirrors! Once again, the officer was completely unsympathetic, eyeing my Indiana driver's license and plates suspiciously. I was angry and accused him of harassing me.

He did let me go, but by that time I was furious. I turned around and went to the Neptune City Police Station to report him. His superior said the guy was a rookie, probably just wanted to be sure I had paid for the first ticket. I told him the whole long, sad story about Danny and that I was homeless. He recommended me to Oxford Apartments and said that I could put his name on the application as a referral.

A one-bedroom apartment was available. When I saw the apartment, I said, "Wow! I'll take it." I had connected with a Christian Church group while working at Perkins, and they helped me move in. Right in front, as I approached the apartment entrance, I saw a statue of the Blessed Mother. The statue belonged to an elderly couple, who lived downstairs. Even though I was distraught, unable to think clearly, I knew that statue was a sign that I was meant to be there. A tiny light of hope began to glimmer in my mind, but I was still caught in terrible darkness.

I had a home, yet I still felt I was homeless. I was alone with no Danny and no mom. I settled into my apartment and saw the new year of 2014 with no hope, no faith, no love, no Danny. I had furniture that I brought back from Indianapolis—mostly Danny's. This was my sixth move in a year and a half.

I had found a *real* job as a counselor for Easter Seals. I was assigned to a residence up in Marlboro, New Jersey. It was a house full of adults with mental disabilities. It was more like baby-sitting, but it paid my bills and kept me busy. The job took my mind off what I did not have, and what I had lost.

I did not realize it, but I had come to be comfortable in my "self-pity, poor-me" security blanket that I wrapped around myself like a homemade Afghan. I was so hurt and in so much pain and so angry that all I did was cry, cry, cry. I could not understand why Danny died, why he could not get sober. I still really had no clue about alcoholism. I thought I did. I thought I should have been able to control Danny, and I thought God and the rooms of AA, where he had gone before and after the accident, would do whatever it took to get and keep him sober.

I could not understand why he picked up the alcohol and could not stop. I hated alcoholics. I hated drinking. I was afraid that I too would die. I was terrified of what would happen to me. I was clueless about my own shortcomings. I was enmeshed with Danny and his disease. Even though I went to Al-Anon, I never felt connected. I was welcomed, but it did not feel like home. There was something missing.

I now realize pain has been my life-long companion. Everything, everyone, I loved has either been withheld from me or ripped away. When I was a child, I wanted to get married and have kids. That never happened. I searched for love and acceptance through the religious community and was rejected by the nuns. When I found the love and acceptance I had searched for my whole life in Danny, he was traumatically taken from me.

I hid my pain well behind a smile, a smile others found pleasing. I endured, without complaint. That smile was a cover-up. It was my false identity: cute, compliant Gina with an infectious personality. Danny's death, and the deep depression I experienced because of it, brought me to a place where that smile did not work anymore. I believed with my heart, mind, and soul the ability to heal, forgive, learn to live, and love again was lost.

There would be no more joy, no happiness. I was in a state of doom and gloom, one of the walking dead. I really felt that way. I would never take my own life, but I often wished to go to sleep and never wake up. I would pray at night for God to take me. The next day, when I would wake up, I would express my disappointment, "Shit, I'm still alive!" I do not know how I managed to survive.

My apartment was simply furnished. I did not care what it looked like. I had friends that put up drapes and gave me sheets, and I used those. Everywhere I had little shrines of Danny—his picture here, giant hearts there, candles everywhere. I would pretend that he was knocking on the door, calling, "Hey, Baby Doll, I'm here." I would listen to his voice messages on my phone repeatedly. I barely ate. I would go to work, come home, and cry. I refused to celebrate the first holidays without him, volunteering to work instead. I skipped all holidays for two years.

One thing I did do—I purchased a bench in memory of Danny on the Belmar Boardwalk. They had become available after Hurricane Sandy destroyed the old boardwalk in 2012. People paid for the privilege of dedicating one of the new benches to a loved one. The only spot still open was right across from Tenth Avenue. On that corner of Tenth and Ocean Avenues is a sober club where Danny used to go. How appropriate to put a bench there with a little brass plaque that said, "Miss you and love you my Dannyboy. Sober & Free, Your Baby Doll." Friends from Indiana donated a tree in memory of Danny and Mom in Lake Como around the lake, a block up where they lived.

That was a place where I sat and cried all the time. I would look at the beach, watch the ocean, and scan the horizon where heaven and earth met. Hours I would sit there and ask, "Why, oh why?"

Life continued around me while I was in emotional quicksand. I did not even try to get out of the emptiness, discouragement, suffering, and pain that had become my state of being. I look back today and see the hand of God moving me. At that time, I thought and felt the God I understood was responsible for all my hardship. I hated, resented, and blamed God and wanted nothing to do with

Him. Still, I believed in Him. I cannot explain it any better than that. I was just so angry. I blamed Him for everything bad that had happened in my life from birth on. I believed I would always be the scapegoat, staying in pain, simply existing. I was done with a relationship between God and me.

Actually, God was doing for me what I couldn't do for myself. In an attempt to find answers, to find myself, I walked into an AA meeting at Holy Innocents Church in Neptune. I don't know why I was compelled to come here. It was an open speaker meeting. I did not know anyone there. I sat in the back, filled with anger and tears and resentments.

There were three speakers sharing their stories, but I could not even tell you what they said. After the meeting, a guy named Craig, who has at least twenty years of sobriety, came over and talked to me. I started crying and shared everything about Danny, my life, my pain, my misery. I used to share like that all the time, with whomever I met and wherever I was.

It turned out that Craig had known my Danny. They lived in the same town, Lake Como. Craig was this big, friendly guy, and he gave me a warm hug that was just what I needed at the time. He invited me to the Shore Club.

Chapter 16

The Shore Club is a sober clubhouse that is open all day and has at least six or seven AA meetings a day. It is the very same club that is across the street from Danny's bench on the boardwalk. Craig suggested I attend the closed meeting that meets daily at noon. My immediate reaction, "I don't have a drinking problem." I knew that at closed AA meetings, everyone identified themselves as being alcoholic. He told me I could still attend. All I had to do was say, "My name is Gina, and I have the desire not to drink today."

I went because I wanted to find out why these alcoholics were sober and Danny could not be. I hated all sober alcoholics at the time. I began going to the Shore Club for the noon meeting and sat in the back on the left side, just to listen. I was in so much pain and was so angry that I heard nothing. It was like they were speaking a foreign language. All I did was cry. I must have looked horrible: depressed, lost, pale, and sad. I did not want to talk to anyone. I came and then left following the closing.

Craig introduced me to John C., and I stuck with him. Of course, I shared my story of woe. I was inconsolable. Here it was, over a year since Danny's death, and it was not getting any easier. All I did was go to the noon meeting and work. John C. was always there to comfort me. He would meet with me for coffee. He introduced me to other sober alcoholics. Men and women came up to me, and as time passed, I began staying after the meetings. Of course, I still shared my pain one on one.

In the meetings I held immense grudges. I would sit at the same spot all the time, holding up the wall with the same two guys in front of me. They were sober alcoholics that attended that meeting regularly. They were truly kind to me. I rarely spoke in the beginning. I did not think of myself as an alcoholic. I was someone in pain—horrific pain—who was unconsciously looking for something. When topics like God, acceptance, or gratitude came up, I cringed. I could not grasp those concepts, hated those topics passionately. Whenever I heard a sober alcoholic complaining about something, I thought, *Just thank God you're alive and sober.*

Some people were long-winded, and I would get impatient. I could not believe some of these people had decades of sobriety and were still assholes. I compared everyone with Danny. I did not understand why they were sober and Danny was dead. AA members would talk to me and share. I was still Gina with the desire not to pick up a drink today. Nobody knew who I really was. They did not know I was a former nun. When the topic of God came up, I did not want to hear it.

Whenever someone encouraged me to pray, reassuring me of God's love, my shattered heart throbbed. *No shit God loves me. I was* married *to Him! I know who He is. I have seen miracles as a sister, but they were always for others, never for me.*

I attended meetings on a regular basis. I see now that was how God was working in my life. God was there for me while I ranted and raved about how I hated life. Scripture says, "Walk in another's shoes before you judge them." I do not know anyone who would have wanted to walk in mine. Yet I kept walking in the door to meetings. Eventually, I started to feel safe enough to share a little bit of my pain, my anger.

I was with a group of drunks who were living a sober life or trying to. Some had days of sobriety, some months, some years and even decades. I kept questioning why Danny was never able to get sober and others did. Repeatedly I heard the phrase, "Knowing how to live life on life's terms." I resisted, thinking, *That will never happen to me.*

I began to let down my guard and let others in, while I held onto my grief and self-pity. I was so used to feeling miserable, it had become my identity. Attending AA meetings, I became intrigued. Alcoholics shared how they were living life on life's terms and staying sober one day at a time, no matter what happened to them. I heard the joy and freedom in their voices that my poor, shattered heart was looking for. They had a key to their success, and I was a prisoner of my grief.

I kept going, day after day, meeting after meeting, even though I did not name myself an alcoholic. I still had Danny's shrines all over my place; I was still half-hoping for my Danny to walk through the door. Yet my body kept going to the club and other meetings. I did befriend a few women and men in the meetings, going for coffee, walking on the boardwalk, sitting on Danny's bench.

Was I drinking at the time? Honestly, I do not remember. I know I still *wanted* to drink, but I also remember thinking that if I picked up a drink, I would die. I listened to stories about how others got into the rooms—sometimes through courts, family members, or DUIs.

I compared myself to them. *Nope, that's not me.* Secretly, though, I could identify with their pain, their disappointments, and loneliness. I did not hear anything like my own story, but I heard stories of brokenness, insecurity, and self-loathing.

Month after month, I kept identifying as "Gina with a desire not to drink today." No one said, "You don't belong here," or told me I was an alcoholic. In these rooms there was love and empathy. Members did not always agree on matters, and there were prideful pontificators and religious preachers. I felt uncomfortable at first and slowly I began to feel the love, hope, and faith that made me feel more comfortable.

One gentleman, a sober alcoholic, came up to me and said, "We know your pain, and everyone in the room is joined with that pain. Yet everyone in the room is also joined in recovery and hope."

The seeds were being planted within me, but I continued to hold onto the pain. You could see it in my face. I held onto the idea I was not an alcoholic. *How could I be? I am not like that one or this one.*

One day I went out to Wendy's for lunch with my friend Marge K. I met Marge K in Al-Anon as well as AA. She is a "double winner." She was in Al-Anon learning to cope with a family member's alcoholism as well as in AA, coping with her own alcoholism. By that time, she had at least 30 years of sobriety. This was in March of 2015, two years after Danny's death. I was still mourning and holding onto Danny. During our conversation, she gently and lovingly said, "Gina, you have been coming to the meetings faithfully as well as attending a step-study workshop identifying as desiring not to drink today. Have you ever looked at yourself and your relationship with alcohol?"

I was stunned to hear that. *It is not about* my *drinking. It is Danny...right?* But once again, seeds were planted beyond the pain. From that day forward, I pondered about what she had said.

A month later, the seed that Marge had planted in my heart came forth to blossom. On April 2, 2015, at the 1:30 PM meeting, when it came around to me to identify, I found myself saying, "My name is Gina. I am an alcoholic." It was a small group. People who knew me from the noon meeting were in shock. I was more in shock than anyone else. I looked around and thought, *Who said that? It cannot have been me. I am not an alcoholic.*

With that admission, something inside me changed profoundly. My story of loss, disappointment, and bitterness renewed into a story of hope, love, and faith. My bitter ending of life still unlived changed into a story of recovery and healing. I had spent so much time in dark despair; the light that now shone on my path to the future was changing my vision. A life I never expected or thought I deserved or hoped to be worthy of—a life of peace and joy—opened like a flower on a spring morning.

When Marge put that seed in my heart that day, I looked back on my life. I saw my relationship with alcohol. It had been my best friend, although I never thought of it that way. I could have used the program twenty-five years earlier. But that was not my story. It was not meant to be.

The truth that ran parallel to the story of pain—the truth of my own alcoholism—was lurking in the shadows, cunning, baffling, and insidious. I never even suspected it was there!

In my youth, I did not know any alcoholics. I thought they were bums on the street drinking from a paper bag. My first drink that I can remember was when I was eight years old. One of the youngest in a large extended family, I recall many family parties—birthdays, graduations, weddings, and holiday gatherings. At one party, I remember I asked Dad for a screwdriver. He laughed and said there was one in the garage.

When I was eight years old, I knew a screwdriver was a drink with vodka and orange juice. That is what I wanted. Should an eight year old know what a screwdriver cocktail is? Dad would let me have the cherry from his Manhattan—the cherry soaked in whiskey and sweet vermouth. I loved the feeling that gave me. I was in another place, in La La Land. I was always drawn to my father's drink. I would ask him for a sip, even of his Schaefer beer.

My parents were not alcoholics. Mom liked her wine at dinner, and Dad would have a beer. When there was a gathering, he would have his one Manhattan, even when we went out to a Chinese restaurant, but never more than one.

I was the seventh child, with six older siblings. I remember my sisters Patti and Paula and their friends would play a drinking game called Bizz, Buzz. I always wanted to be part of that group, the older crowd. Even though I was little, they allowed me to join them. I was always smiling, and they thought I was cute.

In hindsight, my relationship with alcohol had formed in childhood. It was a relationship that took me away from myself. It made me the center of attention with my friends. I hid it well from my family, though, from those I loved, especially my parents. I loved them very much and never wanted to hurt or disappoint them. I thought they were on the same level as God. You can imagine, I was one confused pup.

I was insecure and fearful. I wanted everyone to love me. I wanted to be popular among my peers. I emulated my older sisters. My self-esteem suffered from having all those surgeries. I went drinking with my friends. I snuck around because I was underage. My fear of getting caught was washed away as alcohol gave me courage and relief from all my insecurities.

At the age of thirteen, I would invite friends over when my parents were not home. We would raid the liquor cabinet. It was a pretty normal thing for kids of that age to do—experimenting with alcohol, mixing all those different liquors together. What was not normal was that when my friends stopped drinking, I kept going. I did not stop until I was sick, until I was throwing up.

One time, Mom and Dad came home and caught me. They were terribly upset. That made me feel bad, but instead of stopping, I tried to hide it better. I thought it was part of life, how you became an adult. I needed to have that bottle, that drink. My drinking made me part of the cool gang. Alcohol made me feel different about myself. I was part of the "in" crowd, not the little girl who had had all those surgeries, who could not play sports, or was unpopular. That Gina I did not like. She was alone, unwanted.

I did not know anything about reliance on God, loving yourself, being positive, or having healthy self-esteem. It was always "poor me," until I had a drink and then another and another.

Confirmation is one of the holy sacraments. The ceremony aligns you with the gifts of the Holy Spirit. The Catholic Church proclaims you as an adult in the church. All my siblings before me had received the blessing. I made my Confirmation when I was 16 years old because my parents wanted it for me. They had a nice family get-together afterwards. That night I had gone to a Halloween party as a gypsy; I squashed the Holy Spirit with alcohol spirits. I got the spins and was violently ill. The ironic part of it was that there was no alcohol served at the party. I sought it outside, among peers. Mom and Dad got the call to come pick up their drunken gypsy daughter.

My parents were so disappointed. I will never forget when my mom looked me in the eye and said, "I've lost my trust in you."

I tried to keep up the appearance of being good and proper. My smile got bigger, but I was in pain inside. I did not share these feelings with anyone: instead, I used alcohol to self-medicate. Alcohol and deception were becoming my identity.

Like a song you do not want to hear but gets stuck in your head, my mind repeated, *I am no good! Everything bad happens to me.* The self-deprecations began to fester. I knew my family loved me, but I did not love myself. I hid my self-dislike and did not seek another's opinion. I thought it was something different about me, a phase I was going through. I tried to fill that void. I could not explain to myself, never mind anyone else, why I felt the way I did. I hoped it would pass.

I went to college in Connecticut. While my high school classmates went to Ivy League schools, I chose a small school where I could have fun. My definition of fun was drinking. I drank to excess. I justified: *It's college. That's what students do.* Looking back, I realize everything I did revolved around drinking. I was the one who had cheap beer. Piels Light was a standard on a college budget. My best friend alcohol followed me everywhere. The more I drank, the bigger my smile became. Empty beer cans littered my apartment on campus. A college friend built me and my roommate a bar to accommodate our drinking. I drank more than anyone. I drank until I blacked out or got sick, sometimes both. The next day, I did it all over again.

In my sophomore year, I began to frequent bars. I discovered a latent talent for playing pool. I was incredibly good at it. I played every day and night and drank with whoever was there. Everyone loved me. I was petite and cute, with a great smile—a girl who could beat you at billiards and drink you under the table. My winning game technique was to shoot and then take a gulp of beer. By the end of the night, I would have won the tables, and would leave loaded, sometimes with a drunken male in tow.

I repeated that scene consistently throughout my college life. Once again, I was searching for real love and acceptance. I found neither in college. I thought I would find my Prince Charming. My two older sisters had, so why not me? When I graduated, I found myself alone, trying to figure out how to live in the real world when I had no idea what part I was to play in it. I felt like a failure. I never told anyone; but I was afraid to leave my college town. The plan was to return home to Harrisburg, live with my parents, party, and bartend while I looked for a "real" job.

My life-long relationship with alcohol caused me a great deal of emotional pain. I suffered early in life from low self-esteem, and throughout primary school and then my college years, I tried to quench my thirst for attention and love with alcohol and even in the convent. The feeling of never quite fitting in was one aspect of an "alcoholic mind." Looking back now, growing up, I had the "isms" described in the AA and Al-Anon programs. Isms stand for I, self, and me, and include denial, manipulation, fear, and pain, all characteristic of alcoholics. As I matured, so did my disease.

As I went through the process of healing the symptoms of my disease, I saw how it manifested into my personality. I was three people:

The Victim: a tragic person in emotional pain, with a broken heart.

The People Pleaser: always smiling and hiding how I really felt.

The Failure: the "poor me," self-loathing, hurt child.

Alcohol was the great uniter. When I drank, I felt whole. When I did not have alcohol whispering in my ear and coursing through my body, I broke apart into a million pieces.

Chapter 17

My official sobriety date is April 2, 2015. When my journey of recovery began, it was not easy. All the pain, all the hurts and brokenness of my past, everything I was holding onto rushed into my awareness. Truth replaced deception. The discovery that alcohol was not my friend tripled the pain.

The preverbal saying "like ripping off a Band-Aid" comes to mind. It was more like gorilla tape being torn off a third-degree burn. My wound was exposed. I felt raw and fragile when I joined AA.

April 2, 2015. From that day forward, members would come up to me and say, "Finally! You are in the right place. Welcome." They all knew I belonged there right from the start. The wisdom of the rooms is you must admit to yourself this is where you belong.

In reflection alcohol was my friend—a very *possessive* friend that kept a tight hold on me. Drinking is only one symptom of alcoholism. There's manipulation, fear, insecurity, feelings of self-loathing—these are all a part of the alcoholic experience. It is a field day for the Devil. Throughout my life I was paralyzed by the disease and fooled by a false sense of comfort.

I had become a prisoner of my own creation. By the time I came into the rooms of AA, I imagined myself in a concrete room with walls that were thick and cold. In the early years of my life there were windows and light, yet the walls got thicker, and finally there were no longer any windows or doors, no light or growth. Not even a little crack through which I could glimpse a better life.

It took another alcoholic, Danny, to show me what alcoholism really was. It was his death through excessive drinking that finally woke me up. His struggle and death helped me to recognize my own disease. Wanting to help him brought me into the rooms of

AA. Admitting my own alcoholism brought me to my knees, and it was in that state of humility that I will live for the rest of my life.

When I realized and accepted that I was an alcoholic, light started to come in. It did not happen overnight, but eventually, I found light, faith, and hope once again. Today there are no walls, doors, or windows. My life is an open floor plan, renewed and refreshed.

I now understand that the disease of alcoholism was behind all the pain. I fell in love with an alcoholic who opened my eyes to the insidiousness of the disease. My alcoholism was disguised as fear and insecurity. My alcoholic mind claimed relief came in a bottle or can or glass. Those underlying feelings of inadequacy, loneliness, and being unloved and unaccepted formed an identity that created a hell-on-earth existence.

The final blow was finding Danny dead. I gave up on life and I lost all that was good about myself. I never thought there would be light, love, and life beyond despair.

When I became aware I was an alcoholic, I officially became a member of the Shore club. That day my heart opened to the possibility of a new life. My new identity as an alcoholic gave me coping skills to deal with my pain. My recovery gave me strength to confront negative feelings and address my insecurities.

I began to see my true being rather than the false version alcohol gave me. I had to admit to being an alcoholic. I had to connect with that little girl within me, who thought she was running away from all the bad feelings by drinking. I had to see using alcohol to dull my pain and fear was what kept me under the influence of this awful disease. It is a disease that escapes being named a disease, even though it killed Danny and countless others. Alcohol wanted me dead, too.

I put my two feet into the program. I searched for a sponsor—someone I could work the steps with, someone I could allow to witness me opening my Pandora's box. I had been observing a woman, Rachel, for months before I said I was an alcoholic. She was always at the noon meeting. In December of 2014, there was a young girl at the meeting with only three days sober. She was in tears and obviously experiencing great pain. Rachel sat beside her and comforted her, saying, "Let us love you until you can love yourself." I was sitting in the back, leaning up against the left wall, in my own pain and tears. When I heard Rachel say that to that girl, I felt, *Oh my God, she is talking to me.* My second thought, *If I was an alcoholic, I would ask her to be my sponsor.* Four months later, when I finally identified myself as an alcoholic, I asked her. She agreed to be my "temporary" sponsor. "Let's give it a try," she told me. "Call me every day." That was the beginning of working the Twelve Steps. To this day she is still my sponsor.

One of the suggestions for newcomers is to go to ninety meetings in 90 days. I had been going to meetings every day for the last ten months, but as a person who desired not to pick up. Now that I identified myself as an alcoholic and really could no longer drink, I had an insane urge to drink. I *wanted* to drink!

The disease began to lie to me much like an alcoholic lies to others. I told myself my story was not like any other person's story. I did not go to jail. I was not ordered by the court to go to meetings. Plus, I was a former nun. I did not have my last drink on April 1, 2015. There are alcoholics who have their last drink the day before they come into the rooms. Certainly, that was not my case. The flood of feelings that poured into my body once I was ready to accept my alcoholism was overwhelming. I wanted a drink. I needed a drink. I heard the disease encouraging, "Go drink. The pain will go away for a while. You might as well drink and be miserable because you will never be happy."

That was the disease and the lies it kept telling me all my life, only I had never recognized it as alcoholism. How could I be an alcoholic? I was Gina, the girl loved by everybody—everybody, that is, except herself.

When the cat came out of the bag, when the deep, dark secret within me came out, it was the greatest gift that was ever given to me. I did not realize it at the time, but I did what I was told. I went to ninety meetings in 90 days, got a sponsor, began working the Twelve Steps. It is suggested that you try to help another alcoholic. Share, share, and share some more. Most importantly, do not pick up a drink, and go to meetings no matter what.

My first 90 days, I attended two meetings a day, crying, sharing, angry, still holding up that wall. The pain became greater. I kept thinking, *How can I be an alcoholic?* I was still confused, still complaining. I would call my sponsor every day like she asked of me. She listened and she would share her experience, strength, and hope. There was a time in those first 90 days I wanted someone to say, "Stand on your head in the corner, and your pain will go away." I wanted a simple fix.

Something new that I would share at a meeting would cause renewed pain. There were layers to my pain. I still was not smiling. I brought my body to meetings, hoping my mind would follow. That was one of many slogans I heard in the meetings, read in literature, and saw hung on the walls. It was all Greek to me. I would continue to go every day, call Rachel every day, listen, and share. I kept bringing my body. For a while, nothing really clicked. I really did not want to hear about God, gratitude, and acceptance. Still, I followed the guidelines, shared the message, and did what was suggested.

I joined what is known as a home group, Saturday Night Live at 7:00 PM in Belmar. I was given the coffee commitment. Some of the members of SNL had been around from the beginning of the group's formation, over thirty years ago. It was a "speaker meeting" where three recovering alcoholics from another Jersey group would come in to share their experiences, strength, and hope each week.

This happened to be the meeting that Danny and I went to when he was first trying to get sober at the Jersey Shore. He had just gotten out of rehab at New Faith and needed to go to a meeting right away. Since this was an open speaker meeting, anybody could attend. I went with him to support him. He met Gary H. and asked him to be his sponsor. Only a week or so later, Danny went back to drinking. Ironic how SNL has continued to be my home group for the last eight years.

I see now how God was working then, and still is. Now I am sober, working the steps and able to see with my heart, mind, and soul how God was with me every step, transforming my shattered heart to a heart that is happy, joyous, and free. The miracles in AA and in my life continue to unfold one day at a time. Let me show you how my pain turned into joy: a joy, a freedom that I would never have thought would be in my cards. It is possible, and it is true, because all things are possible with God.

Chapter 18

I came in like the walking dead, locked in my own prison. When I was a sister, I was told I could not be angry, so I kept that inside. I had kept all those feelings in ever since I was young. Never complained, never said I was hurting or afraid. I carried all those "isms" throughout my life. Thank God for AA. Thank God for the rooms, the tools, the fellowship, and thank God for God! I never thought it would be possible to be grateful. It did not happen overnight. Coming into the rooms and saying I was an alcoholic was just the beginning. I was a slow learner as I came in, and even working on the steps was slow.

I was still in denial. Certainly, Gina Economopoulos could not be an alcoholic. Not Sister Regina Marie either! For the first ninety days, I was comparing and questioning. After all, I was not a fall-down drunk, and I had never gotten arrested for drinking.

I did get a ticket once when a group of us in high school were caught drinking in a public parking lot. However, I was never in handcuffs, never imprisoned. The only time I ever saw the inside of a prison was visiting the people I served while I was a sister. They were not confined by choice, and once they did their time, they would be released. I chose to enter the walls and could leave at any time. Alcoholism is a life sentence. There are those who come to acceptance of their disease and are even grateful when being sober evolves into sobriety. It can be a beautiful way to live.

In the first year I did the "AA Waltz," steps one, two, three, one, two, three, repeatedly. The condensed version: "I can't, God can, I will let Him." Rachel was always there, picking up the phone and listening with love, always non-judgmental. Still, I questioned if I was really an alcoholic. I knew deep down that if I picked up a drink, I would soon be dead. Drinking helped me escape reality, but someday it would kill me. Those were the thoughts in my head. I was filled with fear and negative thoughts. I heard in the rooms the disease will disguise itself in your own voice.

I pressed forward, spoke with Rachel, made coffee in my homegroup, reached out to other alcoholics, most importantly, did not pick up alcohol. I practiced that one a day at a time. My sobriety evolved with a great deal of tears and resentments. I questioned everything. Time, dedication, and constant reminders like "There but for the grace of God go I" helped me become a sober person.

The worst type of imprisonment is the one I gave myself. I was the judge and jury. I sentenced myself with the help of alcohol and unresolved pain. Before the program, there was no way for me to escape my self-destruction. AA helped me to see the truth. My questioning received answers, and my doubt turned to understanding.

Doing the AA waltz, the first three steps, was perfect for me in my first year. Once I honestly admitted to myself and other alcoholics I was one of them, the healing in those rooms became available to me. There was still a battle within me. I came to meetings and shared my day count—three days, eleven days, etcetera. Sharing it and calling it out made me accountable. Those who had watched me struggle hugged me and said, "Finally, you have joined our club! Welcome!"

I held onto my pain for a long time. The First Step in AA is "We admitted we were powerless over alcohol, that our lives had become unmanageable." I had been trying to control my pain, protecting myself from more pain and disappointments. When I did the First Step, I had to let go of the illusion of protection from suffering that alcohol used to seduce me. The pain stayed bad and even got worse before it got better. My disease tried to convince me that I was not a real alcoholic, that it was okay to have a drink and kill the pain for a while. There were no magic words to turn my darkness to light, misery to joy, pain to healing. It truly was, and is, a one-day-at-a-time program.

I had no social life in early sobriety, and definitely no boyfriend. I spent my free time at the Shore Club. The club and the meetings held there were my safe place. There was a pool table, so I occupied myself with that outside of meetings. I knew when I was in the club, I was surrounded by people who were sober and wanted to stay that way.

I was on a new adventure, a new chapter to find peace, joy, and happiness that had eluded me in the past. It was freedom that my insides were seeking. At that point in my life, there was nowhere to go but up. At first it was Danny's story that brought me into the rooms, but in that first year I realized it was my own alcoholic story that kept me there.

By now you know my pain. Pain so unbearable all I could do was surrender. Throughout my life, I searched for the answer to "Why?" It was not until I walked into the rooms that the answer slowly began to dawn on me. The answer was within.

To drink the pain away was my alcoholic solution. My negative sense of self, the poor, poor, pitiful me story, and the victimhood were to get attention. I was comfortable in having others feel sorry for me. I thought dreadful things only happened to me. When terrible things happened, Gina had to suck it up and not say a word, put a smile on her face, make everything peaceful.

I kept my feelings close as a child, until my mother died. Then I wore my grief, pain, and sadness like a brand. When Jesus came back into my life and I was learning to be a nun, I went back into silent suffering. I was filled with fear but kept it silent. I was told I was suffering for the community like Jesus on the cross. I certainly felt like I had gone through Jesus' passion, figuratively dying and being buried. There was no resurrection for me there, though. It was all about sacrifice and suffering.

Once I left the convent, there was more suffering with Danny. I shared that grief and pain repeatedly with anyone who would listen. My tears flowed without me thinking. Even in my first 90 days, I cried all the time. Without speaking I broadcasted, "Look at me, poor me."

Alcoholics shared in meetings how they came into the rooms in pain. They identified with my suffering and then they spoke of hope and love and new ways of living. I did not hear or did not want to hear life could get better. I sought others who were in the same pain as me.

During that first year, I would often meet my sponsor for the noon meeting at the club. She is a great hugger. Her hugs were a big part of my recovery. Her mantra, "Let us love you until you can love yourself." Everybody knew Rachel. Everyone got hugs from her. When I spoke to her each day to check in and share, she would always listen. She never told me what to do. Instead, she would share her own experiences. If something or someone bothered me about a meeting, she told me to look at my own feelings and to pray for them and myself.

At about 45 days, someone said to me that I did not sound like an alcoholic. That got me questioning myself all over again. *Well, I didn't ruin any relationships with my drinking, did I?* However, I had blackouts in college and could not wait for Sunday to come around for alcohol to be put on the table at the convent. When I was the sister in charge, I would say, "It's Saint So and So's feast day—let's put out the wine or beer at dinner."

I remember that desire to drink. The relief when insecurity and feeling unloved subsided, even if it was temporary. I wanted to be the popular teenage-college girl, bartender, nun, and have everybody love me and accept me. I wanted that attention; I need their approval so I would feel good about myself.

When this guy told me I might not be an alcoholic, I was devastated. The confused me that looked for approval wanted to belong as a recognized member. I felt deceived. After that meeting, I was upset and angry. My sick mind encouraged me, *Go drink and see if you're an alcoholic or not.* It sounded logical. I was in pain, so why not? I went to a local convenience store that sells alcohol. I bought a quart of Blue Moon beer. I loved Blue Moon beer. I felt the power of anger that alcohol enhances. *Let me show him, and myself. Let us settle this question finally.*

We are told in the rooms, before you pick up alcohol, call someone. I was told to call my sponsor. I did not want to call Rachel. At that point, she had twenty-five years of sobriety. I did not want to hear what she would say. Instead, I called a girl I had met at the meeting that day. She was counting days, forty-five, same as me.

She had heard what took place at the meeting. I told her I had a quart of Blue Moon on my counter. She questioned, "Did you call Rachel?"

I answered, "No." My memory of what happened after we hung up is vague. The bottle was still on the counter, and I was in my bedroom when Rachel called. Reluctantly, I picked up the phone.

My friend had phoned Rachel. My sponsor talked to me in a gentle, loving voice. I do not know exactly what she said. I did tell her I was questioning if I was a real alcoholic, and that my brilliant idea was to try alcohol and see. Rachel listened and shared, and the next thing I knew, I was calling Liz and asking if she would come over and empty the bottle out for me. She did. I did not drink that night.

Who knows what might have happened if I had? The disease is so cunning and baffling. The voice of encouragement to drink was my own voice. From that moment forward, I went to meetings knowing I no longer needed to question whether I belonged in AA or not. That was the one and only time I got close to drinking again, just to see if I was a real alcoholic.

The first two years, I wanted a "microwave recovery." I was exhausted carrying that pain. I wanted it to instantly go away. Slowly I began to understand that my solution was in the rooms of AA, listening to others sharing. They all had been where I was, even if the circumstances that brought them into the rooms were different from mine. The empathy and compassion came from a mutual experience of alcoholism.

I heard how the program worked in their lives. I saw the joy and felt the peace that exuded from those we call the winners. I learned that "Time takes Time," and that it stands for "Things I Must Earn." I am Italian and Greek and tend to be impatient by nature. I wanted that peace and joy immediately. It took me time to grasp the meaning of the first three steps.

I struggled with the word "Powerless" in Step One. I did not understand what that meant. It did not click in my mind. I was going to a beginners' Step meeting at the time, and I would question that concept repeatedly.

My alcoholism had been hidden deep in my persona. I buried the symptoms deep in my ego's justifications. The red flags of fear and anxiety fluttered in the winds of my insecurities. I know now that God was caring for me when I could not. It was God's grace that guided me. God knew what I needed when I did not.

He knew the burden was too great for my small self. He has been guiding me and sending me help when I could not do it alone. From the moment of my conception and birth through my final time of rest, I know the Lord is my shepherd. All the events of my life, good and bad, brought me to the rooms of AA. On April 2, 2015, when those words came out, they were simply words at the time. I did not know where they came from, but I am glad I finally said to them, "Hi, I'm Gina. I'm an alcoholic."

When I accepted my disease, I was still not a huge fan of God. I was filled with resentment and hatred. I did not know it was God setting me free from bondage—the self-made prison I had been living in. The journey of sobriety is a journey of faith, healing, and stepping into the light.

I formed a new relationship with my Higher Power, whom I choose now to call "God." In the beginning, God (H.P.) was on the couch. I blamed Him for everything.

Despite how I viewed God, I never stopped believing in Him. I saw the power God bestowed upon his children when I was a sister. The healings, the help for the community, and bringing people back to the Church. For me, God was good for everyone else. For me, He was pain and suffering. Give all the hardships, pain, and suffering to Sister Regina; she would sacrifice and suffer for others.

I felt everything that had happened to me, to Sister Regina, was all God's fault. The way I was born, my physical problems, my mom's premature death from cancer, the cruelty of the sisterhood, the loss of Danny—it was all God's doing in my alcoholic mindset.

The "Why me?" attitude, the resentment, slowly dissipated after I stopped drinking and joined AA. As a member of the Shore Club, having a home group, working the steps with a sponsor, and following good advice, the light came on in my brain without my realizing it. It was an extremely slow process, but it was the right one for me.

I eventually managed to get to Step Two, where I changed my attitude towards God, and Step Three, where I began to trust Him to guide me.

Chapter 19

Rarely would I hear of someone undertaking the Fourth Step early in sobriety. Step Four is taking "a searching and fearless moral inventory of ourselves." It is a step that alcoholics fear, or do not take at all. I was told if a person does not complete Step Four, they will eventually drink again.

In my first year, Step Four was a faraway destination. I was not afraid or concerned about what others might say because I waited. I realize that everyone has their own opinion about staying sober, or even what sobriety is to them.

There are sponsors who encourage their sponsees to work the steps as quickly as they can. There is nothing wrong with that, and there is nothing wrong with slow sobriety. One should work the steps the way they feel most comfortable. For me, I did the first three steps for over a year. I had questions about being an alcoholic. I had admitted my alcoholism, but I had not really *accepted* it. It took me a while, because for me it was an entirely new concept. Friends in college or at the convent might have thought I was an alcoholic or just drank too much, but I was clueless. For me, the first year was learning to accept my alcoholism.

I did so many outgoing speaking commitments with my friend Buddy from the home group. The more I shared my story, the more I became convinced I was an alcoholic. I fought the acceptance part. I struggled with Step One, especially that word "Powerless." Then, one day at a meeting, I heard the word "Surrender."

I imagined a white flag. That is what powerlessness is—surrender! I knew that word from my convent days. We were compelled to surrender. Surrender meant taking the pain in silence. In AA I learned not to be afraid to surrender to the truth. Surrender leads to freedom. My conditioning had the word all twisted. I believed what the convent told me that pain and suffering were my burden to carry in silent servitude to humanity.

I was trying to control everything so I would not get hurt again. I thought that protecting myself by controlling people, places, and things around me was the way to stay safe and have peace. In the AA program I became aware that it was working the steps that would bring me that sense of safety and peace.

They told me, "Stick with the winners." I did. That idea attracted me. I respect everyone's sobriety, but there are those sober people of whom I am not a fan. I resolved to stick with those that had the kind of sobriety I wanted for myself.

(H.O.W.), the **H**onest, **O**pen, and **W**illing slogan, was there from the moment I joined AA. Willingness is the key to living a sober life. Up until now, my life had been full of a certain kind of willingness: I was willing to avoid pain, sidestep suffering, achieve peace at any cost. As a nun, I attended counseling and went to a religious rehab. I was willing and tried different ways to get help where I sensed I needed it.

Every time I had picked up a drink, I was running away. I made progress in counseling and through prayer. For small amounts of time, I found peace in the chapel, or visiting shrines. That peace was from the outside. It did not stay with me. Consistently, I would flee into the bottle, which only added more suffering. I searched and never found the source of my unhappiness because it was the well I drank from regularly.

I look back now and see the well I drank from to live was what was killing me one day at a time. I could have used these rooms in my twenties, but it was not meant to be. Once I realized and accepted my alcoholism, I saw with clarity my reactions and choices were due to my disease.

Being an alcoholic is like being a diabetic. When you are diagnosed with diabetes, you make changes in your life. Food, drinks, sleep, exercise, and even occupation come under scrutiny. *Is this good or bad for me with this condition?* One must have the same considerations when surrendering to alcoholism. I had to make changes like going to meetings, not drinking, and learning to be honest, open, and willing. These are changes that saved my life. The lifestyle change did not cure my alcoholism, but my life became manageable.

In 2015, I had nothing, felt nothing, and believed in nothing. Somehow, in eight years, I went from nothing to something, from darkness to light, from sadness into joy, from an unhealthy solution to curb my suffering to living life on life's terms. Before sobriety, everything was all about me—what life and God were doing to me.

When I stopped taking emotional selfies, I saw a bigger picture. I can appreciate the scenery and embrace life as life. A good friend once said, "Life gets lifey." The good, the bad, and the ugly all are parts of life. This too shall pass; pain comes, and it goes; happiness is fleeting unless you practice it every day.

Learn something new every day; listen with an open mind; live each day as if it is the only day you have. The rooms of AA gave me the peace that I was looking for, the peace that I have today, eight years later. My life is a miracle.

Through the grace of God, and persistence in the program, I approached my first anniversary of sobriety. My heart assured me I was ready. Now it was time for the Fourth Step: "Made a searching and thorough moral inventory of ourselves." It was not my sponsor or anyone in the room who said it was time; it was my heart. I was listening to self-love.

Rachel never pushed me, even as others asked me if I was working on my Fourth Step yet. I would avoid the question, or simply say "No," and walk away. My sponsor, whom I love dearly, blessed me with patience, "As long as you don't drink or drug, it's all good."

I celebrated that one-year anniversary with my home group. I felt light. There was peace. I shared Danny's story. Danny's tragic death pushed me into the rooms. I stayed because I am alcoholic. That is my truth.

When I first heard about the Fourth Step, the concept was not new. In the convent we called it confession, and at least once a year, you would do a general confession, taking responsibility for all your past wrongs. You would confess to a priest after having done a thorough examination of conscience. *Where did I sin? Where did I go against God?*

Once we confessed and received absolution from the priest—forgiveness from God—we were made whole again. That is, until we left the confessional booth, and then something would happen, and we'd experience a negative reaction or an unkind thought, and there you would go, sinning again!

Those are "venial" sins, the Catholic Church would say. Then there were serious "mortal" sins. To die with a venial sin unrepented would not keep you out of heaven. To die with a mortal sin unforgiven would keep you out. We are human, less than perfect, and that is why we turn to God for his grace, mercy, and guidance to be better.

As a sister, I was in confession quite often. I knew my shortcomings. As a nun I did not know I was an alcoholic. Many of my "sins"—my struggles—were "isms" of alcoholism. I blamed everyone else for my fear, self-loathing, and anger. I was treated unfairly, but if I had been in recovery back then, that pain and fear would not have existed. I would not have put up with mistreatment from a sick community.

I was not meant to be a religious sister for my whole life. It was a hardship, a painful experience that my heart, mind, and soul had to go through. It was in recovery that I could integrate the lesson.

I approached Step Four with an attitude. I thought I knew it all, knew myself, knew my character defects. *This will be a walk in the park.* That is what my ego was telling me, and that is why it took me until my second year of sobriety to complete Step Four. It was the right time for me, but not for Rachel. She suggested I find someone that had sufficient experience to function as my "Step Sponsor."

Amy from the Shore Club had five years of sobriety. She agreed to come over to my apartment weekly to go through the steps. We started from the beginning, in the *Big Book of Alcoholics Anonymous,* by reading "The Doctor's Opinion." We also used a book called *The Twelve Steps and Twelve Traditions of Alcoholics Anonymous,* affectionately known as the "12 and 12."

Amy took me through the steps as she was taught, reading the *Big Book*, going through paragraph by paragraph, highlighting, writing things out. Things like "What am I powerless over? Who is God to me?" I had to start over with God. I had experienced intense pain in my past relationship, but there were blessings too. I had been married to the guy for twelve years, so I do know Him. Now, being divorced from Him, I saw that it was a bitter divorce.

I was confused. I pushed myself forward and was as honest, open, and willing as I could be at the time. I was willing to give God another shot. Where else could I go? I was in deep pain. There was no way out except for up. Like you hear in the rooms, you get desperate, sick, and tired of being sick and tired. I was emotionally bankrupt, suffering from a soul sickness that had wiped me out.

Listening and hearing about God again, I had to start fresh. I see now how H.P. had to work slowly and gently with me, going through the step work with Amy. I knew it was not going to be perfect, but I was on my way to becoming a better version of Gina.

Step Four helped me to have compassion for myself rather than pity. I saw my character defects, and I embraced my assets. Step Four is a shift that can only happen after doing the first three. I knew I was powerless over alcohol, and that my life had become unmanageable. I had truly surrendered to those facts and renewed my relationship with the God of my understanding. I was ready to take a good look at myself. To see myself through the distortion my drinking had created. How my behavior affected others and how their reactions influenced my feelings. I had to face what was my part in my list of resentments.

On top of the list was God. Then there was me, Gina. Of course, the sisters' community and the friars. Then there was Danny. Even though he was dead, he was on the list. It was not a lengthy list. I put down those that had hurt me, because that pain was prevalent in my mind and heart. I did put my family down, because I recognized the envy I had towards my siblings since I was a child, as well as Indiana—yes, the state!—where Danny and his mom had the accident.

Part of Step Four was to list your fears. That was a thorough list for me. My top fears were not being in control, being hurt, and being in pain. These fears were constant companions. I tried so hard to control people, places, and situations to avoid being hurt. I thought that was the key to freedom and happiness. But the more I tried to control, the more out of control I felt, the more pain I experienced.

I once heard a holy priest say, "Fear equals control." He gave the example of when the Angel Gabriel came to Mary and comforted, "Be not afraid." In other words, He was saying, "Be not in control." That always stuck with me. My fear came from the feeling of being out of control. My greatest fear was living life with faith as my steering wheel. There were more fears; rejection, betrayal, being unloved, not belonging, insecurity, criticism, shame, the laundry list of the alcoholic.

Writing out my list was a huge relief. The power resentments wield over you in your mind lessen when you put them on paper. It is like something lurking in the shadows that comes to light. The truth, no matter how bad it is, can be healed whereas the lie needs to stay in the dark to fester. Getting real with yourself begins the healing process. At first all I could see were my negative character defects. As I embraced them, I started to see a different perspective about my true character.

I learned my defects stemmed from negativity I experienced in childhood. I modeled the behaviors I thought would please others. I had two separate lives. The one I showed and the one I kept secret. I thought no one could see the darkness in my soul. God did. God forgave me even before I sinned, because he had made me and knew as a human I would stumble.

With God's grace I got back up and learned from my mistakes, faced my fears, and vowed to do better. As a sober woman, it was hard to look at these defects of character. Although I felt I had already done this work, it was an entirely new way of healing when I did it through the Twelve Steps. I did have a spiritual experience. It was not religious, and that is what the people in the program stress. This is not about religion. I needed to rethink all those religious thoughts, that religious way of life, because it was not working. Pain and suffering are not requirements of a sober life.

I was still fragile and had to go slowly or I would have turned and run away from the pain of self-examination. Once I learned what my defects were, and began to embrace them, healing happened naturally. I took responsibility for my actions and reactions, saw and accepted my part in situations.

Everything stemmed from fear, the need to control, selfishness, my ego, my pride. I was ashamed to admit that at first because I had been hiding behind false Gina with the eternal smile. False Sister Regina, always smiling. As a nun, I was told that I could not be angry, especially at other sisters, and it took time to unravel that falsehood, that misconception that had taken hold of me.

Step Four was a step of courage to write down and take ownership of what I had done, of what I had not done, and to bring goodness and healing to those situations and relationships. The list of defects from my Fourth Step—impatience, shame, negativity, and selfishness—I realized this is not the true me.

The version of me as seen through my defects was the result of untreated alcoholism. I am not my defects, and I am not a mistake. I define my character by my actions today, and my God does not make mistakes. I am a work in progress. Life became gentler when I lightened up on myself. Life will go on with or without me. My journey continues with God as my compass.

One of the requirements of Step Four, as set forth in the *Big Book*, is to look at your sexual conduct. How did I treat the men in my life? In college, I was promiscuous. I learned in recovery that I did not respect myself, my body, or the men I shared it with. I was insecure.

When I became a nun, I made vows of obedience, celibacy, and poverty. Celibacy is when you renounce marriage and any sexual relationship with a man. It means you vow to give your whole heart, body, and soul to God. Celibacy in religious life is a supernatural grace.

For twelve years, every day, I chose God and the grace to stay chaste. It was difficult. There were times I wanted physical affection. I did not have any sexual pleasure, money to spend as I wished, or control over my life, and I was very lonely. Alcoholism and my character defects were stirring up during that time.

I completed Step Four with all my resentments, fears, and sexual inventory put down on paper. I had learned at the convent that you do not dig for stuff. It will come up through God's grace. In the convent I believed I had examined and forgiven myself and others. I was not sober, or in recovery, and did not even know I was an alcoholic.

Discovering my alcoholism and entering a recovery program was the answer to all my problems and pain. The Fourth Step, although difficult, became one of the best tools in my healing toolbox. It turned pain into joy.

I looked at my defects through the lens of AA, which suggested I write down my assets. Others saw me as kind, compassionate, and spiritual. I always knew I had a heart of service. I was never into material things. I lived simply, helping others, and putting myself last. I did everything with a big smile. Deep down I was desperately unhappy and uncomfortable. I had no self-love.

In my Step Four inventory, I realized there were aspects of my personality that helped me stay alive through my trials. I had perseverance and was stubborn, with a tendency to hold on, no matter what. God worked with those assets to help me survive. Faith, hope, and love were there; they were just overshadowed by my harsh reactions to negative experiences. Positive thoughts have come alive in me. Sobriety is a gift, a priceless treasure. Miracles happen all the time, and I am one.

My sober life has given me a new relationship with my Higher Power, whom I call "God." My spirituality has opened my heart. Through God's grace, I have aligned with a moral compass. Honesty, openness, and willingness are part of my daily habits. To be sober, know myself, and be comfortable in my own skin is precious. To love and be loved unconditionally is heaven on earth.

Chapter 20

Step 5 states that we admit to God, to ourselves, and to another human being the exact nature of our wrongs. This step is like confession when you tell your sins to a priest in contrition and vow to do better with God's strength. In the program, I shared my defects and wrongdoings with a faithful, trustworthy friend.

That was hard for me. I did not trust anyone, especially women, because I had been abused by the women in the religious community. Once I admitted and acknowledged all those defects of character aloud, I was free. I could separate the good from the bad and choose what to keep and what to let go of.

Step Six is where we become entirely ready to have God remove all these defects of character. It sounds like a simple step, but it can be hard to do. Letting go of the false identity I had developed was like trying to fit a square peg into a round hole. From childhood I had accumulated maladjustments that skewed my thinking, until I found sobriety. Alcohol had been the only solution to deaden the pain and frustration.

When I was in the bottle, my fears went away. The warmth I felt as alcohol coursed through my body made me feel loved and accepted. I felt a sense of belonging. I was convinced it was the cure to my suffering. Once I woke up—or came to—the next day, all those negative feelings were right back with regret and shame added to the mix.

Making this step meant I had to be ready to lose all my former "friends"—those negative and unhealthy coping skills. It is scary. In Catholic confession, the priest tells you God has forgiven you and that you are to go forth and sin no more. But we are human. We are going to screw up again, no matter how hard we try. I saw that in the convent, where the peace of reconciliation with God might only last until the next negative encounter with another sister.

Step Six is intrinsically different. We are being asked to give all our defects to God, trusting that they will be removed in His suitable time. It takes away the inevitability of failure and adds an element of release—not only from the defect itself but from the responsibility for healing it. I was ready to have all those character defects removed. I was ready to start a new, healthy way of living. I had accepted my alcoholism and was making new friends among the alcoholics I met at meetings. We have a common denominator: We do not need or want to live in hell anymore.

Step Seven is closely related to Step Six and requires a specific action, a change in attitude towards ourselves and how we move in the world. It says, "We humbly asked God (as we understood God) to remove our shortcomings." I took this step in my own living room, alone, on my knees. I read my list of defects aloud to my God. I believe with all my heart that He heard me. I also gave Him my assets, because they are who I truly am—a Child of God. I will never be perfect. All I can hope for is a healthier way to deal with my problems, with God's help. I no longer escape my feelings in a bottle, or anywhere else for that matter. God oversees my healing. I am a sober, faithful woman today, walking in the light and the truth. I can grow and heal. Anything I must do to maintain my sobriety is totally worth it!

Chapter 21

What is this "magic" that is Alcoholics Anonymous? Is it some secret society where you must know the special handshake to get in? Does it cost money? Are there any guarantees?

In the beginning of a typical AA meeting, first we say the serenity prayer, then one will hear three readings from the *Big Book*. The *Big Book* to an alcoholic is like the Holy Bible to Christians. Reading and following the suggestions of the *Big Book* saves many alcoholics who want to get and stay sober.

First is the preamble, which welcomes the alcoholic and states that we are not alone. We have a common problem of alcoholism, yet we have a healthy solution in the rooms of AA. It also states to keep our sobriety is to give it away by helping others.

The second reading shares how the program works, and it includes the Twelve Steps. To sum it up, for an alcoholic to find and keep sobriety is to find a higher power to clean house and to enable them to help others. The alcoholic cleans house by going through their own inventory, listing their character defects and the wrongs they have done to others. Through God's grace and the suggestion of their sponsor, in time, they reach out to ask for forgiveness and make amends with those they hurt while actively drinking. As one follows these steps, they will comprehend the word "serenity" and know peace, one of twelve promises that an alcoholic experiences as they stay sober one day at a time. The promises are a vision of what life can be like if we follow this simple spiritual program.

We (alcoholics) will always have the disease of alcoholism. We are never "cured." We recover by working the steps, going to meetings, not picking up the first drink, and by helping another alcoholic. These actions help us arrest the disease one day at a time. It is work. It is the exact opposite of everything active alcoholics do. AA is a place to look at yourself, to live your life daily in sobriety. Some days are harder than others.

The first three steps can be summed up in the acronym "**H.O.W.**," which stands for **H**onesty, **O**penness, and **W**illingness. This reading addresses the fact that some people are incapable of being honest with themselves—a human condition. The honesty required in Step One is key, and it is the only step I had to do perfectly. Everyone has their own journey to get to that step, but I was told not to compare the differences in our stories.

When you attend meetings, over time, you will eventually hear your own story. It might not be exactly the same, but you can identify with the feelings. That identification is critical. It really helps to know someone else has gone through what you have, has felt the way you did, and has found a path to recovery. The commonality of our stories is what holds us together in recovery. We all know that continuing to drink, or going back to it, only leads to jails, institutions, and death for the alcoholic. The disease always gets worse, never better, unless you seek help.

Why stay in recovery? It is that new freedom and new happiness that the alcoholic has been seeking their whole life and finds through working and eventually living the Twelve Steps. There are many promises that one receives as long as they stay sober and work the program.

When I first heard the promises, it was hard. I thought, *Nope. Those will never happen to me. Yes, for everyone else, but not me.* The only one that registered with me was the last one: "God is doing for us what we could not do for ourselves." I hung onto that one. It made sense to me. It was not me that was going to get me sober. I was the living dead. Today, eight years later, the promises have all come true for me because I worked the program.

I entered the dark pain of my soul with my H.P. and faced my disease with His help. This was not the "microwaveable sobriety" I had been seeking when I was new. I faced my resentments, admitted I was holding onto my pain and listening to fear, and acknowledged the harm my sexual conduct had inflicted upon myself. I needed to be reconciled by forgiving God, myself, and all the others. By embracing and accepting that it all took place—the good, the bad, and the ugly—I was healed and reunited with the God of my understanding. He comforted the little girl inside me that was consumed by fear, pain, and hurt.

I completed my step work by making a list of people I had harmed. For Step Nine, I became willing to make amends to them. These people came from my resentments list in Step Four. For example, I wrote a letter to Danny, apologizing for being mean, threatening to leave him, and not being there for him. I read it to him at his grave site. I continued to monitor my behavior with Step Ten. In Step Eleven, I worked on my relationship with God, and in Step Twelve I carried the AA message to other alcoholics through speaking commitments and service work.

There is no "graduation" from AA step work—you continue to practice these principles daily, using the program to guide you in a lifetime of sobriety.

As a result of this step work, there is freedom today in my heart. I would say that I am about 90 percent healed. A couple of weeks ago, I was talking to a friend. She shared something with me that triggered pain and frustration with the friars and sisters.

When that grudge and frustration was stirred up, I questioned, *Why the hell am I holding onto it so deeply? They do not care. It is not affecting them, only me.* They say in the rooms that our resentments keep us bound up. Those we resent are getting on with their lives, completely unaware of how we feel. I decided to let it go by saying the Resentment Prayer that is found in Chapter 14 of the *Big Book*.

When you have a resentment, pray for the person or situation, asking God to give them all the grace that you want for yourself. No, you do not pray for their punishment or revenge! You do it daily for two weeks, no matter how you feel about it.

At the end of the two weeks, when I finished the prayer, I got a message from none other than Sister Maria in my voicemail. I was in shock! The prayer worked. She said she was thinking of me, and wanted to talk to me, and that she loves me very much. She said, "Please forgive me if I've done anything at all to make your life so hard." She wanted me to forgive her, and to know that she is praying for me, and she loves me. She left her phone number in case I wanted to call her back. Here is another example of how God is working in my life, fifteen years after I left the convent.

My emotions swirled. I saw how close I am to God and realized that I had indeed forgiven her. There was the sign. Another lesson is I do not need to call her back—today or ever. I feel good about that. What I learned in the program is acceptance. Just take it as it is.

Hearing her voice brought me back to the old days, more in an uncomfortable way than a painful one. I cannot explain the joyful sense of freedom I experienced after the call. I can accept her apology, but I do not have to talk to her or have coffee with her. I do not trust her. I do not need to trust her. I can continue to live my sober life joyous, happy, and free.

I know that call was a gift from God, for me as well as for her. If there are any more steps I need to take, God will show me. Once again, the old Gina would have called her right back and said, "No worries—oh, you didn't do anything wrong." My people-pleasing character defect would have come out full force if I had not done that work in Step Four seven years ago.

There is peace in my heart now. I do not relive that pain or resentment. Life is good for me today, and each day it gets better. Most of the time I forget I was a sister and what took place in the community. The bad memories do not occupy my daily thoughts. I even forgot that whole experience about being a murder suspect and had to be reminded by someone who knew it was part of my story.

Chapter 22

Along with healing, joy, and new friendships, God in his goodness has given me someone incredibly special in my life—Brian J. I met Brian early in my sobriety. I was sitting on Danny's bench, right across from the Shore Club, watching the sunrise before the 7:00 AM meeting. He strolled down the boardwalk and sat down beside me. We talked and discovered we had much in common. He too was counting days and was from a family of eight children.

Brian lived in Westchester but was vacationing with his family in Spring Lake for a couple of weeks that summer. He walked to the 7:00 AM meeting every morning, and that is where we became friends. He was going through a divorce, and I was still grieving for Danny.

Our friendship developed slowly. I told him his sobriety came first, then his family. I would not demand to be first in anyone's life who was trying to get and stay sober. I focused on my own sobriety and grief. Brian helped me work through my grief.

The first time Brian came to visit me in my apartment, I had shrines to Danny everywhere. He never once criticized me or asked what was wrong with me. He was very compassionate and understanding. It was my own decision to put the Danny shrines away and let Brian into my life.

From the beginning, we were amazingly comfortable with each other. We talked and talked. Three years later, Brian moved down to the Shore, and we committed to a relationship. It took trust for me to have a relationship. I was working on the program and had a sponsor who I talked with daily. I learned my experience with healthy relationships was limited. Brian was helping me with that too. He had his own struggles with alcoholism, and he is sober today and works a great program.

When the right time was right, I was introduced to his family, his sons and former wife. It was amazing how they welcomed me. The kindness and acceptance they showed me was appreciated. When his former wife entered the rooms of AA, we knew what a blessing this was for everyone. We share the common denominator that we are alcoholics, living life free from alcohol and drama daily.

Brian and I are living together now. We have a great sober life. His former wife, as well as his former mother-in-law, are in the program today. It is one big family of love, faith, and joy. What a difference to be in a family that is not only sober but has this program. There are times we are on the same AA Zoom meeting together, laughing and sharing. As a matter of fact, this past Saturday night, April 27, 2024, they were both on Zoom with us celebrating my nine years of sobriety. It is a miracle, and everyone we know bears witness to the love we share. I know from the bottom of my heart that Danny somehow brought us together so I could experience sober happiness, joy, and freedom.

Afterword

M any, including myself, have been hurt by those who claim to be doing God's work. Today I do not blame the people who choose to leave the church. They have their reasons, and I respect their choice.

Throughout the world there is so much pain. We are coming out of the COVID-19 pandemic, and a great deal has changed. The news makes everything worse; I see fear and pain everywhere. There are people suffering from natural disasters and human-caused trauma. There has never been a greater need for hope.

Sunday, July 2, 2023, I got to share my experience, strength, and hope at a speaking commitment. I sign up for AA speaking commitments frequently. Each time I speak, there is tremendous passion in my heart and my voice about this program. I always include my story of pain, disappointment, and loss, as well as the healing I have found in recovery. The reason is, each source of pain, each loss, each disappointment and hardship, has shaped who I am.

I had received many gifts of sobriety. Now, each morning, I am grateful that I woke up alive, I am sober, and I have a God in my life. Everything that comes after that is a bonus. I learned through the tools of the program, prayer, and reading scriptures that I am able to live life on life's terms instead of running towards a drink or heading into a deep dark of misery.

So many can identify with feeling like shattered glass. Something that cannot be fixed and must be thrown away. I never dreamed I could be restored to life the way this program has restored me. My past with its sorrows, pain, and loss cannot be changed, but I can choose to take what I like about myself and leave the rest behind. I am becoming a better version of myself. Not only can I love God, myself, and others; I am able to love Brian and receive his love fully and freely. Now I have a daily purpose—to stay sober and help another alcoholic to achieve sobriety.

On Monday October 10, 2016, at 5:15 PM, my dad, whom I was very close with, died unexpectedly from a heart attack in the Milwaukee Airport with my two sisters by his side. I spoke to him daily when he lived with my sister JoAnn. When I received that call that evening, I immediately called another alcoholic and went to a 6:30 PM meeting, where I shared my pain and cried to those that were there. I was able to grieve in a healthy way, not the way I grieved with Mom and Danny. AA has taught me there is hope in grieving without picking up a drink to numb the pain. It sounds strange, but I am so grateful to be an alcoholic, to live a happy, joyous, and free life that I participate in in a healthy way. I miss my dad, mom, and Danny, but I also know that they are smiling upon me and continue to love me.

Something else—something extra special—has come out of the painful experiences of my life. I discovered through ministering to the poor in the Bronx as a Franciscan Sister that I have a unique ability to comfort the terminally ill. As a person passes through the last stages of life before succumbing to their disease, I can listen, empathize, and bring a peaceful presence to their experience. The very natural process of dying can be transformed into a healing, loving time of spiritual completion, and in my new career as a certified end-of-life doula, I feel certain that I am fulfilling one of my God's designs for me.

Acceptance is the answer to all my problems. I learned that in the rooms, and it was a tough pill for me to swallow. I had to let go of the resentments that defined me and to accept everything that had happened as having been necessary to get me into sobriety. In the five stages of grief, Acceptance is the last stage after Denial, Anger, Bargaining, and Depression. When you have accepted the past, embraced it, and given it to something or someone greater than yourself, healing can begin.

This wonderful smile God gave me no longer hides anything. My heart has been healed. There are scars, yes, but my heart knows who I am and is now filled with only love. I am so grateful that God has been with me throughout my journey. I now know that He was always beside me—in my childhood, at the convent, with

Danny, and during my struggles with recovery. Without these experiences I would not be who I am today—a sober woman of faith with a purpose to give Him all glory and honor. At my celebration of nine years last week, someone pointed out how God used me to touch others in the convent yet now God is using me even more in the rooms of AA.

Never thought of it that way, but I totally agree. This is who I am, an alcoholic who is sober, and with my experience, strength, and hope I can help others.

A final word about alcoholism: It is an incurable and fatal disease. However, with total abstinence and support from others in recovery, alcoholics can find a daily reprieve from this deadly and insidious condition and live a happy and useful life.

If even one person reading this book can find hope from my story of pain and redemption, then my telling it will have been worthwhile. Take courage, find a Power greater than yourself, place yourself in the hands of that Power, and find the light. You are a miracle waiting to happen, just like me.

Life goes on....

Danny's Bench, where heaven and earth meet.

Meet Gina

Born and raised in the vibrant community of Syosset, New York, Gina Economopoulos emerged as the seventh child in a family of eight whose roots were deeply intertwined in an Italian and Greek-loving family. She grew up in a Catholic traditional upbringing with unconditional love from her parents.

Despite facing numerous surgeries from a young age, each shaped her into the resilient individual she is today. With a degree in social science from Eastern CT State University, she ventured to Harrisburg in 1989, where she seamlessly blended her social work background with bartending, embodying the essence of hospitality.

Following the loss of her mother to cancer in 1992, she embarked on a spiritual journey that led her to the convent for twelve years before caring for adults with disabilities. Settling on the tranquil shores of the Jersey Shore in 2010, she encountered love and loss, finding solace in sobriety through Alcoholics Anonymous.

Today, as an end-of-life doula, she extends her compassionate heart to those in their final chapter, grounded in faith and guided by the wisdom of the scriptures. She is also very much involved in the rooms of AA in service and reaching out to other alcoholics. While enjoying simple pleasures like playing golf, shooting pool, traveling, or going to the beach, she navigates life's journey with gratitude and grace, forever grateful for the blessings that adorn her path.

A Note From Gina

Step into Gina Economopoulos's world beyond the pages of *Shake the Dust Off Your Feet and Walk*. Delve into her enduring journey of resilience, faith, and compassion as she navigates life's twists and turns. Stay connected for updates, blogs, and more on her website, www.GinaEcon.com, and embark on a captivating voyage of inspiration and connection.

Follow her on her journey of healing and self-discovery, and celebrate a life of peace, freedom, and self-love that might not have been possible without the losses and suffering she endured before.

Made in the USA
Middletown, DE
11 September 2024

60206029R00084